Coping With the Seasons

✔Treatments *That Work*™

Coping With the Seasons

A COGNITIVE-BEHAVIORAL APPROACH TO SEASONAL AFFECTIVE DISORDER

Therapist Guide

Kelly J. Rohan

OXFORD

UNIVERSITY PRESS

2009

OXFORD
UNIVERSITY PRESS

Oxford University Press, Inc., publishes works that further
Oxford University's objective of excellence
in research, scholarship, and education.

Oxford   New York
Auckland   Cape Town   Dar es Salaam   Hong Kong   Karachi
Kuala Lumpur   Madrid   Melbourne   Mexico City   Nairobi
New Delhi   Shanghai   Taipei   Toronto

With offices in
Argentina   Austria   Brazil   Chile   Czech Republic   France   Greece
Guatemala   Hungary   Italy   Japan   Poland   Portugal   Singapore
South Korea   Switzerland   Thailand   Turkey   Ukraine   Vietnam

Published by Oxford University Press, Inc.
198 Madison Avenue, New York, New York 10016

www.oup.com

Oxford is a registered trademark of Oxford University Press

Library of Congress Cataloging-in-Publication Data

Rohan, Kelly J.
Coping with the seasons : a cognitive-behavioral approach to seasonal affective disorder :
therapist guide / Kelly J. Rohan.
    p.   ;   cm. — (TreatmentsThatWork)
Includes bibliographical references.
ISBN 978-0-19-534108-9
1. Seasonal affective disorder—Treatment.   2. Cognitive therapy.
I. Title.   II. Series: Treatments that work.
[DNLM: 1. Seasonal Affective Disorder—therapy.   2. Cognitive
Therapy—methods.   3. Psychotherapy, Group—methods. WM 171 R737c 2008]
RC545.R64 2008
616.85′27—dc22

                                                                    2008017766

9   8   7   6   5   4   3   2   1

Printed in the United States of America
on acid-free paper

To my parents, Betty and John F. Rohan, Jr.

About Treatments *ThatWork*™

Stunning developments in healthcare have taken place over the last several years, but many of our widely accepted interventions and strategies in mental health and behavioral medicine have been brought into question by research evidence as not only lacking benefit, but perhaps, inducing harm. Other strategies have been proven effective using the best current standards of evidence, resulting in broad-based recommendations to make these practices more available to the public. Several recent developments are behind this revolution. First, we have arrived at a much deeper understanding of pathology, both psychological and physical, which has led to the development of new, more precisely targeted interventions. Second, our research methodologies have improved substantially, such that we have reduced threats to internal and external validity, making the outcomes more directly applicable to clinical situations. Third, governments around the world and healthcare systems and policymakers have decided that the quality of care should improve, that it should be evidence based, and that it is in the public's interest to ensure that this happens (Barlow, 2004; Institute of Medicine, 2001).

Of course, the major stumbling block for clinicians everywhere is the accessibility of newly developed evidence-based psychological interventions. Workshops and books can go only so far in acquainting responsible and conscientious practitioners with the latest behavioral healthcare practices and their applicability to individual patients. This new series, Treatments *ThatWork*™, is devoted to communicating these exciting new interventions to clinicians on the frontlines of practice.

The manuals and workbooks in this series contain step-by-step detailed procedures for assessing and treating specific problems and diagnoses.

But this series also goes beyond the books and manuals by providing ancillary materials that will approximate the supervisory process in assisting practitioners in the implementation of these procedures in their practice.

In our emerging healthcare system, the growing consensus is that evidence-based practice offers the most responsible course of action for the mental health professional. All behavioral healthcare clinicians deeply desire to provide the best possible care for their patients. In this series, our aim is to close the dissemination and information gap and make that possible.

This therapist guide applies cognitive-behavioral therapy (CBT) for depression to the treatment of seasonal affective disorder (SAD). The prevalence of winter-type SAD is significant, especially at higher latitudes; even more common is subsyndromal SAD (S-SAD) or milder "winter blues." Dr. Rohan provides a much-needed treatment for SAD in a complete and accessible package. The therapist guide outlines a 12-session group program to be conducted over 6 weeks during the fall or winter. It may also be used with individual clients or in conjunction with light therapy (LT). Participants learn effective CBT techniques that will serve them this winter and beyond. The protocol consists of psychoeducation, behavioral activation, cognitive restructuring, and relapse prevention. The corresponding workbook follows the program session-by-session and provides forms for homework. Specifically tailored for use with the SAD population, clinicians will find this a unique and beneficial program for their clients.

David H. Barlow, Editor-in-Chief,
Treatments *ThatWork* ™
Boston, MA

References

Barlow, D. H. (2004). Psychological treatments. *American Psychologist, 59,* 869–878.

Institute of Medicine. (2001). *Crossing the quality chasm: A new health system for the 21st century.* Washington, DC: National Academy Press.

Acknowledgments

First, I would like to acknowledge the contribution of all of the participants in the Seasonality Treatment Program, formerly at the Uniformed Services University of the Health Sciences (USUHS) and now at the University of Vermont, who have made this work possible and rewarding. The development of a cognitive-behavioral therapy (CBT) treatment for seasonal affective disorder (SAD) would not have been possible without decades of prior work by others on the cognitive theory and therapy of depression and on the behavioral conceptualization of depression and behavior therapy. For this, I am most grateful to Aaron T. Beck and his colleagues, particularly Judith S. Beck, in developing the theory and treatment principles that inspired me to modify cognitive therapy for SAD and to Peter M. Lewisohn and his colleagues for developing pleasant events scheduling as a potent behavioral treatment strategy that has proven very useful for SAD. These treatment components represent much of the material contained within this manual, and their originators deserve full credit for them. I would also like to thank Alan Peterson for sharing his ideas on basic psychoeducation regarding depression symptoms and relapse prevention. I am grateful to my colleagues, David A. F. Haaga and Teodor T. Postolache, and to my former clinical graduate students and co-therapists, most notably Kathryn A. Roecklein, Kathryn Tierney Lindsey, and Brenda Elliot, who provided helpful feedback on the content of this program at the time it was initially being conceptualized and tested. Thanks also to the National Institute of Mental Health (NIMH) and to the USUHS for funding the clinical trials that have tested this protocol to date.

Contents

Chapter 1   Introductory Information for Therapists   *1*

Chapter 2   Group Logistics   *15*

Chapter 3   Session 1: Introduction to the Group   *21*

Chapter 4   Session 2: Symptoms, Prevalence, and Causes of SAD   *29*

Chapter 5   Session 3: How Activities Relate to Mood and Thoughts   *39*

Chapter 6   Session 4: Doing More to Feel Better   *47*

Chapter 7   Session 5: What You Think Influences How You Feel   *57*

Chapter 8   Session 6: Cognitive Distortions   *67*

Chapter 9   Session 7: Evaluating Your Automatic Thoughts   *77*

Chapter 10   Session 8: Rational Responses   *83*

Chapter 11   Session 9: Core Beliefs   *91*

Chapter 12   Session 10: Evaluating Your Core Beliefs   *99*

Chapter 13   Session 11: Maintaining Your Gains and Relapse Prevention   *107*

Chapter 14   Session 12: Review and Farewell   *115*

Fidelity Checklists   *121*

References   *135*

About the Author   *139*

Chapter 1 | *Introductory Information for Therapists*

Background Information and Purpose of This Program

This guide presents a cognitive-behavioral group treatment for seasonal affective disorder (SAD). The treatment is based on an integrative cognitive-behavioral model and represents a tailoring of traditional cognitive-behavioral therapy (CBT) for depression to the special needs of the SAD population. CBT is placed in a seasonality framework, recognizing the role of environmental changes as well as cognitions and behaviors.

The session-by-session protocol for conducting 1.5-hr CBT sessions twice a week over 6 weeks (total of 12 sessions) is described in this guide. To be implemented effectively, this program is recommended for educated mental health professionals (e.g., psychologists, psychiatrists, and social workers). Some prior training in cognitive-behavioral approaches is also recommended because this manual, in itself, does not teach providers how to do CBT and assumes a basic proficiency in conducting cognitive therapy.

This treatment was designed as a group program, and this guide is addressed to the group leader(s). See Chapter 2 for more information on group logistics. Although we have not tested our treatment using an individual therapy format, we believe that the content of this manual could be easily adapted for use in individual therapy.

Seasonal Affective Disorder

SAD is a subtype of recurrent depression that involves a regular temporal pattern in the onset and remission of major depressive episodes

(MDEs) at characteristic times of year (Rosenthal et al., 1984). The substantial majority of cases are winter-type SAD, defined as recurrent MDEs with a regular pattern of onset in the fall or winter months and remission in the spring. A small minority of cases are summer-type SAD, with regular MDE recurrence in the summer. Winter-type SAD is the focus of this guide, and the term *SAD* will be used to refer to winter-type SAD hereafter. In the *Diagnostic and Statistical Manual of Mental Disorders, Fourth Edition, Text Revision (DSM-IV-TR)*, SAD is diagnosed as major depression, recurrent, with seasonal pattern (American Psychiatric Association, 2000; see Table 1.1 for seasonal pattern specifier diagnostic criteria). The *DSM-IV-TR* also includes a diagnosis of bipolar I or II disorder with seasonal pattern (i.e., bipolar-type SAD), which is not the focus of this guide.

DSM-IV-TR MDE criteria represent the spectrum of SAD symptoms. The majority of SAD patients endorse depressed mood, loss of interest or pleasure in activities, and persistent fatigue (Magnusson & Partonen, 2005). In contrast to nonseasonal major depression, SAD patients more frequently endorse (a) hypersomnia than insomnia and (b) increased appetite, excessive carbohydrate craving, or weight gain than decreased appetite or weight loss (Magnusson & Partonen). Other atypical depressive symptoms, not contained within the *DSM-IV-TR* criteria but common in SAD, include an afternoon or evening slump in mood or energy and reverse diurnal variation (Lam, Tam, Yatham, Shiah, & Zis, 2001; Rosenthal et al., 1984). Seasonality, the tendency to vary across the seasons in mood and behavior, differs in degree across individuals, and full-blown clinical SAD symptoms appear to represent an extreme along a continuum of human seasonality (Kasper, Wehr, Bartko, Gaist, & Rosenthal, 1989; Rosen et al., 1990).

SAD characterizes 10–20% of recurrent depression cases (Blazer et al., 1998; Magnusson, 2000). In population surveys of U.S. adults, SAD prevalence generally increases with latitude and ranges from 1.4% in Florida to 9.9% in Alaska (Booker & Hellekson, 1992; Rosen et al., 1990). Subsyndromal SAD (S-SAD)—defined by moderate changes with the seasons and commonly referred to as the "winter blues"—is even more common than SAD and ranges in prevalence from 2.6% in Florida to 19% in Alaska.

Table 1.1 Seasonal Pattern Specifier Diagnostic Criteria

- There is a regular temporal relationship between the onset of MDEs and a characteristic time of year.

- Full remissions (or change to mania or hypomania in the case of bipolar-type SAD) occur at a particular time of year.

- In the last 2 years, major depressive episodes that demonstrate these temporal seasonal relationships have occurred.

- Seasonal MDEs substantially outnumber nonseasonal MDEs over the lifetime.

- There is no obvious seasonally linked psychosocial stressor responsible for the seasonal pattern.

Available data suggest that the long-term course of SAD is variable. In a review of four longitudinal follow-up studies of SAD patients; Lam et al. (2001) concluded that 28–44% of these SAD patients later developed a nonseasonal pattern of depression recurrence or incomplete summer remission, 14–38% went from having SAD to S-SAD or into remission, and 22–42% continued to have "pure" SAD (i.e., winter depressive episodes and complete summer remission).

The cause of SAD is yet to be established, but several hypotheses have been proposed: phase-shift, photoperiodism, photon-count, and serotonin. See Session 2 for summaries of each of these hypotheses.

Development of This Treatment Program

The central public health challenge in the overall management of SAD is prevention of depressive episode recurrence over subsequent fall or winter seasons. Therefore, the major impetus for developing this particular treatment program was the identified need for a SAD treatment with the following qualities:

1. a time-limited treatment (i.e., acute treatment completed in a discrete period versus daily treatment every fall or winter indefinitely),

2. a treatment that effectively treats acute SAD symptoms in the initial winter, and

3. a treatment that shows effects that endure beyond the cessation of treatment to prevent the annual recurrence of winter depression.

Although light therapy (LT), the established and best available treatment for acute SAD, clearly fulfills criterion 2 for acute efficacy (Golden et al., 2005; Terman et al., 1989), it does not fulfill criterion 1 or 3. For acute and long-term SAD management, available clinical practice guidelines recommend daily use of LT, from onset of first symptom through spontaneous springtime remission, during every fall or winter season, generally spanning 3–6 months of the year (Lam & Levitt, 1999). Therefore, LT, by definition, is not a time-limited treatment (does not meet criterion 1) but instead is a palliative treatment that presumably works by suppressing symptoms so long as treatment is ongoing and must be continued with regularity over each fall or winter season to have continued efficacy (does not meet criterion 3). Currently available alternative treatments to LT have the same problems (see section "Alternative Treatments").

There would be no need to develop a treatment with these three qualities if SAD patients continued using palliative treatments such as LT with good compliance over subsequent winter seasons. However, that does not appear to be the case. A retrospective follow-up survey of SAD patients treated at the National Institute of Mental Health between 1981 and 1985 revealed that only 41% of patients continued regular use of LT (Schwartz, Brown, Wehr, & Rosenthal, 1996). When queried as to why they discontinued using LT, perceived "ineffectiveness" and "inconvenience" were the two most commonly cited reasons.

We believe that a CBT[1] tailored to SAD has potential to fulfill all the three criteria described earlier. Cognitive therapy (A. T. Beck, Rush,

---

[1] Our decision to call the treatment *cognitive-behavioral therapy* rather than *cognitive therapy* reflects our theoretical stance that the behavioral treatment components such as pleasant activity scheduling directly target overt depressive behavior, in its own right, as a primary mover to effect change in depression and that the cognitive treatment components such as cognitive restructuring directly target negative cognitions, in their own right, as a primary mover to effect change in depression. However, our treatment protocol is a revision of A. T. Beck et al. (1979) cognitive therapy for depression, tailored to SAD.

Shaw, & Emery, 1979) is a time-limited treatment that is acutely efficacious for nonseasonal depression and appears to confer benefits that extend beyond the point of treatment termination (Gloaguen, Cottraux, Cucherat, & Blackburn, 1998; Hollon, Stewart, & Strunk, 2006). Several studies have found that depressed patients who demonstrated a clinical response to cognitive therapy had a reduced risk of depression relapse as compared to patients who initially responded to antidepressant medications (Blackburn, Eunson, & Bishop, 1986; Evans et al., 1992; Hollon et al., 2005; Simons, Murphy, Levine, & Wetzel, 1986). In addition to reducing the more proximal risk of relapse, a recent trial found that patients who had fully recovered from the episode treated with cognitive therapy demonstrated a reduced risk for a wholly new depressive episode onset (i.e., recurrence) relative to patients who had fully recovered from the initial episode with pharmacotherapy (Hollon et al., 2005).

Cognitive-Behavioral Model of SAD

Our conceptual model, referred to as the integrative, cognitive-behavioral model, provides a theoretical rationale for this treatment. In an expansion of M. A. Young's (1999) dual-vulnerability model, our proposed model maintains an emphasis on a dual (i.e., physiological and psychological) vulnerability to SAD, but adds depth and breadth by specifying a role for cognitive and behavioral factors in contributing to the psychological vulnerability. According to our model, SAD episode onset occurs when environmental changes activate a reverberating cycle between the psychological and physiological vulnerabilities or when anticipation of winter activates the psychological vulnerability, which, in turn, activates the physiological vulnerability. Thus, the psychological vulnerability factor has maintenance, and possibly onset, etiological significance.

The cognitive component of the psychological vulnerability factor (A. T. Beck, 1967, 1976) includes maladaptive schemas, attitudes, and automatic thoughts typical of nonseasonal depression, but adds environment-specific thoughts related to the winter season, light availability, cues that the seasons are changing, and weather. Our model further incorporates another cognitive component, ruminative coping (Nolen-Hoeksema, 1987), as well as behavioral factors such as a low rate of response-contingent positive reinforcement (Lewinsohn, 1974) and learned emotional and psychophysiological reactivity to low light- and winter-relevant stimuli in the environment. Preliminary studies have associated automatic negative thoughts (Hodges & Marks, 1998; Rohan, Sigmon, & Dorhofer, 2003), dysfunctional attitudes (Hodges & Marks), rumination (Rohan et al., 2003; M. A. Young & Azam, 2003), a negative attributional style (Levitan, Rector, & Bagby, 1998), and reduced pleasant event frequency and enjoyment (Rohan et al.) with SAD. Our CBT protocol targets these cognitions and behaviors to improve acute SAD symptoms and to prevent episode recurrence.

As our model illustrates, perhaps LT is an insufficient treatment for some individuals with SAD because a purely biological explanation is incomplete. LT targets the physiological vulnerability factor, but does not directly address the psychological vulnerability. CBT, however, directly targets the hypothesized components of psychological vulnerability. In addition, the combination of cognitive-behavioral therapy and light therapy (CBT + LT) would intervene at the level of both vulnerabilities.

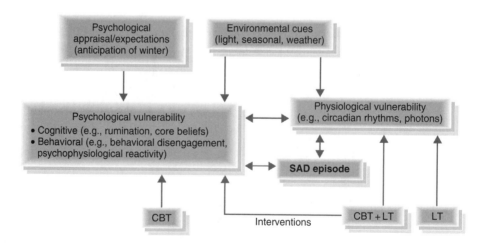

Figure 1.1

Integrative Cognitive-Behavioral Model

Our protocol uses traditional elements of CBT such as behavioral activation and cognitive restructuring to promote improved coping with the winter season. Some cognitive restructuring exercises focus on challenging negative thoughts related to the winter season in general, low light availability, seasonal cues in the environment, and weather. Owing to the predictable nature of SAD recurrence, relapse prevention can be more specifically targeted in SAD than is possible in nonseasonal depression. Our relapse-prevention treatment component emphasizes early identification of negative anticipatory thoughts about winter and SAD-related behavior changes, using the skills learned in CBT to cope with subsequent winter seasons, and development of a personalized relapse-prevention plan to enhance treatment durability.

As mentioned earlier, this program consists of 1.5-hr group CBT sessions twice a week over 6 weeks (total of 12 sessions). Although CBT for depression is typically administered for 12–20 weekly sessions, SAD necessitates an intensified version. With winter lasting just 3 months, SAD patients would spontaneously remit with the arrival of spring if CBT were to be conducted weekly over 20 weeks. Each session typically begins with a review of the previous session and the "homework" assignment and concludes with a preview of the next session. There is a great deal of summarizing to reinforce learning, and we recommend that the reviews be done in question-and-answer format to be interactive.

The protocol (see Table 1.2) starts out in Week 1 (Sessions 1 and 2) with some basic psychoeducation about SAD and depression, including a rationale for using CBT for SAD. Week 2 (Sessions 3 and 4) focuses on behavioral activation using pleasant activity scheduling. This is presented as a means to get out of "hibernation mode" and a way to develop wintertime interests. Weeks 3–5 (Sessions 5 through 10) focus on cognitive therapy. This work involves education about the cognitive model, using thought diaries to record automatic negative thoughts, Socratic questioning to evaluate negative thoughts,

Table 1.2 Summary of Sessions

Week	Sessions	Component
1	1 and 2	Psychoeducation
2	3 and 4	Behavioral activation
3	5 and 6	Cognitive therapy
4	7 and 8	
5	9 and 10	
6	11 and 12	Relapse prevention

generation of rational responses, and an exploration of core beliefs. Week 6 (Sessions 11 and 12) focuses on maintaining gains and relapse prevention.

Evidence Base

Preliminary data from two randomized clinical trials in our laboratory suggest that our CBT may be an effective treatment for acute SAD and that initial treatment with CBT may have superior outcomes when compared to initial treatment with LT the next winter season. In our feasibility randomized trial of 23 community adults who completed 6 weeks of study treatment, CBT alone, LT alone, and the combination of CBT and LT all significantly improved symptoms across the 6-week trial on two different measures of depressive symptoms (Rohan, Tierney Lindsey, Roecklein, & Lacy, 2004).

Based on the feasibility study, we could not rule out the possibility that apparent treatment effects were due to the passage of time or regression to the mean. Because a larger sample size and true control group were needed to replicate the preliminary findings regarding CBT for SAD, we initiated a controlled, randomized clinical trial. The study randomized 61 community adults with SAD to CBT, LT, combination treatment, or a concurrent wait-list control (i.e., a minimal contact/delayed LT control; Rohan et al., 2007). Those who received CBT, LT, and combined treatment experienced significant and comparably improved depression severity relative to the wait-list control in intent-to-treat and completer samples. CBT combined with LT (73–79%) had a significantly higher remission rate at the end of treatment than the wait-list control (20–23%). These findings suggest that CBT, alone or combined with LT, holds promise as an efficacious SAD treatment and warrants further study.

Because we believe that preventing SAD episode recurrence over future winters is a more important outcome than acute treatment efficacy in the initial winter of study, we used our pilot data to examine longer-term outcomes. We conducted an intent-to-treat analysis of outcomes during the subsequent winter season (i.e., January or February of the next new winter season; approximately 1 year after acute treatment) using all 72 participants randomized to CBT, LT, and combination treatment (24 CBT, 25 LT, 23 CBT + LT) across our two pilot studies (Rohan, Roecklein, Lacy, & Vacek, submitted). We used multiple imputation to estimate next-winter outcomes for the 17 individuals who dropped out during treatment, were withdrawn from protocol, or were lost to follow-up. The CBT (5.8%) and combination treatment (5.2%) groups had significantly smaller proportions of winter depression recurrences than the LT group (39.2%). CBT, alone or combined with LT, was also associated with significantly lower interviewer- and patient-rated depression severity at 1 year as compared to LT alone. Among completers who provided 1-year data, all statistically significant treatment group differences persisted after adjustment for ongoing treatment with LT, antidepressants, and psychotherapy.

There are several aspects of these studies that differ from clinical practice. In both of these randomized trials, inclusion criteria for participants were (a) aged 18 or older, (b) *DSM-IV* criteria for Major Depression, Recurrent, with Seasonal Pattern, and (c) a current SAD episode. Exclusion criteria were (a) current psychiatric treatment (i.e., psychotropic medications, LT, or psychotherapy), (b) another current Axis I disorder, and (c) bipolar-type SAD. In both studies, the principal investigator (PI), a licensed psychologist with expertise in SAD and experience in CBT, provided the study treatment alongside a clinical graduate student cotherapist. These studies were conducted in the Washington, DC, metropolitan area, with sample demographics as follows: 93% women, mean age $= 47$ years ($SD = 12.6$), 81% Caucasian, 75% college educated, 79% currently employed, and 49% currently married. Therefore, it is not known whether these findings generalize to SAD patients with comorbid diagnoses or bipolar-type SAD or to SAD patients who are also concurrently involved in other treatments, to professional interventionists other than the PI, and to samples with different demographic characteristics.

Risks and Benefits of This Treatment Program

The benefits of this treatment program to participants include the possibility of improving across the course of acute treatment and the possibility of continued benefits from treatment over the next winter season and possibly beyond. We believe that the risks to participants associated with this treatment program are minor. There are no known negative side effects to CBT. However, it is possible that some individuals may not feel comfortable discussing or thinking about personally sensitive information or events during the group CBT sessions. Some individuals prefer individual to group therapy. Some individuals may find it inconvenient to attend the twice-weekly therapy sessions over the 6-week course of this program and/or to complete the "homework" (i.e., self-help) assignments between meetings. Participants who cannot fairly consider any possible role for nonbiological factors in SAD and/or any nonbiological treatment option may not be appropriate for this program.

Alternative Treatments

LT, a minimum of 30 min of daily scheduled exposure to 10,000 lux of cool-white or full-spectrum fluorescent light with ultraviolet rays filtered out, is recommended as the first-line treatment for SAD (Lam & Levitt, 1999). Available treatment options for SAD include LT and antidepressant medications, both of which are supported by evidence from several studies, and newer treatments that show promise, such as dawn simulation and negative ions (Westrin & Lam, 2007). Aerobic exercise has also shown promise as an acute SAD treatment in a preliminary investigation

(Pinchasov, Shurgaja, Grischin, & Putilov, 2000). These treatments are palliative treatments that presumably work by suppressing symptoms so long as treatment is ongoing. Therefore, patient preferences and the likelihood of adhering to a daily treatment regimen during the symptomatic months each year warrant careful consideration in selecting a treatment plan.

The Role of Light Therapy and Medications

For clinical use, we believe that this CBT program can be combined with LT in a synergistic effect to maximize acute treatment efficacy. This is based on our data that CBT combined with LT had the highest post-treatment remission rate in our randomized clinical trial (Rohan et al., 2007). Our model conceptualizes SAD as a multifaceted disorder with both physiological and cognitive-behavioral factors involved in the onset and maintenance of symptoms. This protocol was designed to present a rationale for CBT that compliments, and does not compete with, the rationale for LT. However, in our pilot studies, only four participants (two treated with solo LT and two treated with CBT + LT) reported any ongoing use of LT at follow-up the next winter. If this finding generalizes to clinical practice, the majority of patients who are treated with combination treatment may not persist with continued LT on their own past the first winter and, therefore, may require explicit instructions to rely on proactive use of their CBT skills to cope with future winters and/or additional treatment to address long-term compliance with LT.

Because internal validity was of primary importance in testing our new CBT for SAD treatment, our preliminary clinical trials excluded individuals who were currently taking antidepressant medications. To increase sample size, we ended up allowing three participants on stable doses of antidepressants into the feasibility study (one randomized to each of the three treatment conditions). Conclusions cannot be reached on the basis of such small numbers, and more data are needed to determine whether the preliminary outcomes for CBT for SAD generalize to individuals taking stable doses of medications. CBT for SAD has not been tested against medications in a head-to-head comparison to date.

Assessment

Before enrolling a participant in this program, we recommend a thorough evaluation to ensure that the individual has SAD. Consistent with the principles of CBT, we recommend administering an objective outcome measure on a weekly or session-by-session basis during the treatment program. We recommend using the Structured Interview Guide for the Hamilton Rating Scale for Depression—Seasonal Affective Disorder Version (SIGH-SAD) (Williams, Link, Rosenthal, Amira, & Terman, 1992) and/or the Beck Depression Inventory—Second Edition (BDI-II) (A. T. Beck, Steer, & Brown, 1996) to measure depressive symptom severity. The BDI-II is a 21-item measure of depressive symptom severity that captures many of the atypical depressive symptoms common in SAD and can be quickly and easily administered before sessions. The SIGH-SAD is a semi-structured interview that includes the 21-item Structured Interview Guide for the Hamilton Rating Scale for Depression (HAM-D) and a supplementary eight-item subscale to assess atypical depressive symptoms associated with SAD. The following criteria define SAD episode onset or recurrence (Terman, Terman, & Rafferty, 1990): total SIGH-SAD score $\geq$ 20 + HAM-D score $\geq$ 10 + atypical score $\geq$ 5. Remission at treatment endpoint can be classified by satisfying one or both of the following SIGH-SAD criteria (Terman et al.): (1) pre- to post-treatment reduction in total SIGH-SAD score $\geq$ 50% + HAM-D score $\leq$ 7 + atypical score $\leq$ 7 and (2) HAM-D score $\leq$ 2 + atypicalscore $\leq$ 10.

Use of the Client Workbook

The workbook for participants follows the treatment program, with each chapter corresponding to a session. The beginning of each chapter lists goals and gives an overview of what participants can expect to learn in group. Session elements are then summarized; participants are encouraged to review the corresponding workbook chapter after each group meeting. Each session chapter ends with a list of homework assignments. Forms are included in the workbook to help participants apply new skills, such as weekly plans for pleasant activity scheduling and thought diaries for cognitive restructuring. Participants should bring workbooks to every session to facilitate homework review and group discussion.

Chapter 2   *Group Logistics*

Forming a Group

Adult participants should be recruited for this group program on the basis of having seasonal affective disorder (SAD), their willingness to participate in this treatment program, and their availability to attend the majority of sessions. We have successfully conducted cognitive-behavioral therapy (CBT) for SAD with groups of participants who vary widely in age. Although it may be desirable from a group cohesion perspective to have same-sex group members, this will not likely be feasible as the majority of our participants (90%) have been females. We have successfully conducted CBT for SAD groups with no or only one male in the group. We have observed that regardless of age or gender, participants generally form a cohesive group around their common experience with SAD.

Group Size

Based on our experience conducting these groups, the ideal group size is four to six group members, with no more than eight per group. This number ensures an adequate balance between the group leaders presenting new didactic material and group discussion or homework review. Groups of four allow for more individual attention and more thorough processing of each member's homework. With a group size of eight, group leaders will not be able to thoroughly review homework from every member at each session and will need to ensure equal time to each member across the course of the program.

Each of our past groups had the same two group leaders throughout the program. We recommend two group leaders, if possible, to help change the focus of attention frequently within each session and to keep discussions going. However, we believe that the program can be successfully conducted by one group leader.

Group Meetings and Program Duration

This CBT for SAD program consists of twelve 1.5-hr sessions, delivered twice per week over a 6-week period in the fall and/or winter. The full 12-session program should be started by early February and completed by early March at the latest to avoid running into spontaneous springtime remission. At Southern locations, it may be necessary to start and end even earlier, depending on when spring arrives. The scheduled meeting time and days for the group should be consistent for the duration of the program. There should be at least 1 day in between the twice-weekly sessions. For example, we typically ran a group on a Monday/Wednesday schedule or on a Tuesday/Thursday schedule. It is important to agree on optimal meeting days and a meeting time slot that works for everyone.

The 6-week period should generally be continuous; however, given the large number of federal and religious holidays in the wintertime, groups may wish to break at one or more mutually agreed-upon times and then resume after the break. For example, we made it a policy not to hold any group sessions between Christmas Eve and New Year's Day because we found that the vast majority of participants were not able or willing to come in during that time. In the event of a scheduled break, it will be important to prepare participants to plan to keep using the skills learned to date over the break rather than taking a complete "vacation" from treatment. This is especially important for SAD because unstructured time can perpetuate winter depression through low activity level and rumination. Group leaders should also have a plan in place for how they will handle any snow days and should make participants aware of that plan. For example, we made it a policy to decide about canceling a scheduled session because of inclement weather as early in the day as possible and for the group leaders to call all participants in the event of a cancellation.

Because the 12 sessions progressively build on one another, it is essential that participants progress through the program in sequence. Therefore, this program is delivered in a closed-group format. In some cases, it is permissible for a participant to join a group in progress in the second or third session if one of the group leaders reviews the missed session(s) with the participant in detail ahead of time, especially group format, rules, and confidentiality from Session 1. Similarly, if a participant must miss one or more scheduled sessions, it is essential that one of the group leaders meet with the participant to review the missed material and ensure that the participant has a clear understanding. If the absence is anticipated, it is ideal to conduct the review ahead of time, although it can be done after the participant returns.

SAD patients frequently elect to travel South in the winter. These trips can be disruptive to the group in several ways. Other group members who are aware of the trip may think that they are missing out on a vacation South and feel disappointed. For the individual participant who travels South, there is a disruption in group attendance that interferes with learning the material in sequence. In addition, assuming the trip is far enough South, patients generally experience a temporary remission of SAD symptoms while away, followed by a return of symptoms within a few days of return from the South. This contrast can be difficult for some people. If the group leaders are aware that a participant is contemplating a trip, we encourage a discussion with him or her outside of the group around the costs and benefits of traveling versus not traveling. We do not advocate that SAD patients set aside money to use for spontaneous trips South when they deem a trip is needed because doing so positively reinforces the depression and negatively reinforces taking trips South in the winter (e.g., the contingency, "If I feel bad enough, I get to go to Florida for a week," increases the chances that one will become more severely depressed and increases the probability of future trips to escape winter). If winter trips South must be taken, they should ideally be scheduled in advance and before symptomatic [e.g., putting the contingency for a trip on an external stimulus (i.e., a date) rather than an internal stimulus (i.e., how badly one feels)].

Maintenance or Follow-Up Sessions

This program, as designed, does not include maintenance or follow-up sessions because it operates on the assumption that once participants complete the program, they keep using the skills on their own to cope with future fall or winter seasons. We have not tested whether follow-up sessions add any benefit above-and-beyond the 12-session format. However, we can see the possible clinical utility of one or two follow-up sessions with participants just before the next wholly new fall or winter season begins to reinforce the skills learned and prepare for relapse prevention. The content of Sessions 11 and 12 would be particularly relevant for follow-up.

Group Rules

The basic rules that group members are expected to follow include confidentiality (e.g., using first names only, not discussing personal information disclosed by other group members outside of the group), mutual respect (e.g., providing equal time in discussions and not interrupting when another member is speaking), arriving on time and staying until the session ends, and calling a group leader ahead if unable to attend a meeting.

Role of Group Leaders

Mental health professionals (e.g., psychologists, psychiatrists, and social workers) with some prior training in cognitive-behavioral approaches are appropriate group leaders. The role of the group leaders is to provide the didactic information outlined in this manual, structure the sessions, offer observations where appropriate, promote interaction among group members, and provide social support. The two group leaders work in a collaborative relationship with each other toward accomplishing these tasks. In advance of every session, it is recommended that the group leaders meet briefly to review the session content and to divide up the didactic material in a way that will frequently change the focus of attention from one to the other. After each session, it is recommended that the group leaders meet to discuss their impressions of how the session went and to problem solve any difficulties specific to the group. The fidelity checklists included in an appendix may be used as part of a supervision process or to rate self-adherence. You may photocopy checklists from the book.

All forms are provided in the workbook and participants should bring their workbooks to every session. For forms that are used more than once (e.g., Thought Diaries), group leaders may want to provide additional copies to participants. You may photocopy these forms from the workbook.

Chapter 3 | *Session 1: Introduction to the Group*

(Corresponds to session 1 of the workbook)

Materials Needed

- Nametags

- Flip chart or writing board

- Copy of client workbook

Outline

- Set agenda (5 min)

- Introduce group leaders and members (15 min)

- Review the goals of this group (15 min)

- Explain the purpose of this group (5 min)

- Discuss the issue of confidentiality (5 min)

- Introduce cognitive-behavioral therapy (CBT) (15 min)

- Discuss changes that the group members can expect to make (15 min)

- Present the rationale for homework (10 min)

- Assign homework (5 min)

Setting the Agenda (5 min)

Begin the session by setting the agenda and writing it on the flip chart. Tell group members that today you will provide them with an overview of the group, its goals, and what they will be working on over the next 12 sessions. You will also describe the kind of treatment this group will be using—CBT. Tell the group that first, however, you would like to do some introductions.

Introductions (15 min)

Introduce yourself as the group leader. You may want to mention your background and experience. Next, have group members introduce themselves (first names only). It is helpful for members to wear nametags. Have members include in their introductions something about themselves; for example, where they are from, what they do, or what their interests are.

Goals of This Group (15 min)

Present the following goals of this group using the dialogues in italics.

1. Increase knowledge and understanding of seasonal affective disorder (SAD). Understand common signs and symptoms and what may cause SAD.

    Having seasonal affective disorder (SAD) means regularly experiencing symptoms of depression each fall and/or winter season that improve with the arrival of spring. It's important that you understand what the symptoms of SAD are so you can recognize them when they occur. This helps you to realize when you are getting better and when you are getting worse. This also allows you to notice when your symptoms are starting before they get really bad. Recognizing symptoms early on means you can do something to interrupt them and prevent them from getting a lot worse.

2. Learn how common SAD symptoms are.

    We'll review the prevalence of SAD and SAD-like symptoms at different latitudes. We'll emphasize that SAD symptoms happen on a continuum, where most people experience them to a certain extent. In other words, most people experience some changes in their mood or behavior with the changing seasons, although the severity of these symptoms differs from person to person.

3. Learn skills to help you cope better with seasonal changes.

    We would like for you to think of the arrival of the fall/winter season as a life circumstance or event that precedes (or comes before) your depressive symptoms. We will be focusing on the way you typically cope with winter and teaching you new ways to cope with the arrival of fall or winter that will be more helpful. We can't change the fact that winter will arrive every year, but we can work to change the way you cope with it. You will learn and practice skills to help you manage, reduce, or eliminate seasonal symptoms.

4. Learn skills to help you prepare for SAD symptoms before they start so you may be able to lessen their impact or even prevent them over future winter seasons.

    You will develop a long-term plan to cope with SAD so you'll be ready for it next year and every year after that. As we've mentioned, recognizing your SAD symptoms early on is part of this plan. It's also important to do something about those symptoms early on before they get worse. It is even better to try and prevent these symptoms before they start; this is called "relapse prevention."

Purpose of the Group (5 min)

You can use the metaphor of a "driving instructor" to explain how this group works:

When you are learning how to drive a car for the first time, you usually have a driving instructor sitting next to you, telling you what to do, and even hitting the brakes if needed. Eventually, you develop your own driving knowledge and rely less and less on the instructor until you finally become an independent licensed driver. You can think of this group as your driving instructor. We will teach you skills that you can use to manage your SAD symptoms. We will give you a lot of guidance at first. After the group, you will be your own therapist. You will know how to recognize your SAD symptoms and have a plan in place to deal with them.

Explain that this is a skill-based treatment group—not a process, encounter, or support group. Tell group members that rather than just talking about their problems, they will learn skills to deal with them. This may be different from other groups they have been in. Emphasize that the group will be interactive. In every meeting, you will ask them questions about their experience with SAD related to the skill they will be learning that day. The group will also talk about how to apply the skills to members' everyday lives.

Ask group members to be courteous to the other group members. You will try to provide participants with equal time to share ideas, ask questions, and discuss any difficulties in using the various skills.

Confidentiality (5 min)

Explain that this group will be more beneficial if everyone can feel comfortable discussing things without worrying that others will find out. To help with this, ask that everyone keep the information discussed in group confidential. In other words, they should not discuss anything about other group members outside of the meeting. You may want to use the following dialogue:

It might be tempting to discuss the group with your family and friends. That's okay as long as you don't talk about other group members or personal things said by other group members. Is this acceptable to everyone?

Obtain group consensus for confidentiality of all personal information revealed by group members before moving on to the next section.

Tell the group that research has identified some of the most effective nondrug treatments for depression, including the types of skills that are part of this program. Explain that this group will use a CBT approach:

> *"Cognitive" refers to thinking and "behavioral" refers to behavior or things you do. It makes sense then that cognitive-behavioral therapy focuses on changing your thinking and your behavior to help you feel better emotionally.*

Inform the group that this program is based on research that has shown that people with SAD participating in a CBT group improved as much as those who used light therapy (LT) over the winter. Furthermore, there is evidence that people with SAD who participated in CBT were less likely to have their SAD return and experienced less severe symptoms in the next winter season compared with people with SAD who used LT in the winter before. In other words, prior exposure to CBT may have some long-lasting benefits for SAD compared to prior exposure to LT.

Based on three decades of research, all of the following statements are true of CBT:

1. CBT is effective in treating both mild and more severe depression.

2. Most comparisons have shown CBT to be as effective as medications in treating depression.

3. CBT has no known adverse physical side effects.

4. CBT may prevent or help delay relapse (or return) of depressive symptoms in the future better than other forms of treatment for depression.

5. Preliminary studies suggest that CBT may be as effective as LT in treating SAD and that prior treatment with CBT may prevent the return of SAD in the next winter season better than prior treatment with LT.

Tell group members that the benefits they will receive from this program depend on their willingness to keep an open mind and try new things. Some changes they may make through this group include becoming more active and thinking more positively (see sample dialogues).

1.   Becoming more active.

Individuals with SAD tend to withdraw or "hibernate" during the fall and winter months. Therefore, they don't do things they would normally enjoy doing—things that are fun. This tends to make SAD even worse. Not only are you suffering from your SAD symptoms, but also you are cutting yourself off from enjoyable activities that may boost your mood a bit. In this group, you will learn how to increase your frequency of pleasurable activities in the winter to improve your mood. When you feel a little bit better, you should have even more energy to do fun things.

2.   Thinking more positively.

Just like those with nonseasonal depression, people with SAD tend to think very negatively. During the fall or winter, it is like they are seeing the world through dark glasses which make everything seem pretty bad. People with SAD also tend to spend a lot of time thinking about how badly they feel and often anticipate their symptoms before they even start. Most of you are probably familiar with that sense of dread or foreboding you get about the winter season before it even gets here. Sometimes the end of summer or seeing things like leaves changing color or days getting shorter can set this off. Again, this way of thinking tends to make SAD symptoms even worse. In addition to thinking negatively about the winter and the weather, SAD is also associated with thinking negatively about yourself, daily situations, other people, and the future. This way of thinking helps keep you down.

Explain that this group will help members understand how the way they think relates to how they feel. They will learn to identify and challenge negative thinking in order to improve their mood. They will also learn to think more positively (or at least less negatively) about the winter season.

Rationale for Homework Assignments (10 min)

You may want to present the rationale for homework assignments using the analogy of learning to play a new sport. Ask the group what are the things they might do if they wanted to learn something new, like how to play golf or tennis. If not mentioned by the group, list these:

- Try it on your own

- Buy a book

- Get a video

- Take lessons

- Practice

Emphasize that practice is necessary to learning something new, whether it be a sport or the kind of skills taught in this program. This program will include "homework" to practice the skills reviewed in group. This homework is practical and meant to help them feel better.

Inform group members that they will not be graded or evaluated on this homework; you just ask that they try their best. In general, the more effort they put into homework assignments, the better they will feel. People who do not do the homework will probably not benefit much from this group. Research actually shows that people who do the most homework in CBT for depression improve the most, regardless of how depressed they were at the start of treatment. You may want to sum up with the following dialogue:

> *It does not matter if we are the best therapists in the world or if the information presented in this group is excellent if you don't practice what you learn here outside of the meetings. Remember our driver instructor/student driver analogy? These homework assignments will allow you to practice your skills between sessions. We and the other*

group members can give you suggestions about how to make the most out of your homework assignments.

Homework (5 min)

✎ Have group members complete the Identifying SAD Symptoms form.

✎ Have group members review Session 1 of the workbook.

✎ Have group members read the overview of Session 2.

Chapter 4

Session 2: Symptoms, Prevalence, and Causes of SAD

(Corresponds to session 2 of the workbook)

Materials Needed

- Group members' completed Identifying SAD Symptoms forms

- Nametags

- Flip chart or writing board

- Copy of client workbook

Outline

- Set agenda (2 min)

- Review content of Session 1 (5 min)

- Discuss SAD and its symptoms (40 min)

- Introduce the vicious cycle of SAD symptoms (10 min)

- Explain the prevalence of SAD (5 min)

- Present possible causes of SAD (15 min)

- Discuss the importance of psychological factors in maintaining SAD (10 min)

- Assign homework (3 min)

Setting the Agenda (2 min)

Begin the session by setting the agenda and writing it on the flip chart. Refer to the outline at the beginning of this chapter and add any other topics particular to the group.

Review of Session 1 (5 min)

Remind group members that in the last session you gave an overview of what this group will be like. Discuss any questions they may have. Review the following points:

1. Group members will be learning skills to help them cope better with the fall or winter season. We cannot change the fact that winter rolls around every year without exception, but we can change the way we cope with its arrival.

2. The kind of therapy we are doing is called cognitive-behavioral therapy (CBT). It is a tried-and-true treatment for depression, with three decades of research to back it up. Evidence over the last several years suggests that CBT may also be helpful in treating SAD and may have benefits that extend into the next winter season.

3. Some of the changes that participants can expect from this group include:

    a. *Becoming more active.* Group members will learn to fight their tendency to hibernate and will begin to engage in activities that they enjoy in order to feel better and have more energy.
    b. *Thinking more positively.* Group members will learn ways to view things in their lives and the winter season less negatively and more positively.

SAD and Its Symptoms (40 min)

Discuss with the group why it is important to start out by talking about common signs and symptoms of SAD:

- To become aware of and understand the different types of symptoms

- To understand how to know when SAD is getting better or worse (symptoms increase or decrease)

- To be able to recognize symptoms early on when they are just starting

Group members may not be aware of all the symptoms of SAD. By recognizing the different types of symptoms, they may better understand the way SAD affects them. Paying attention to when symptoms increase and decrease can help members track their progress. Early intervention in symptoms can prevent SAD from becoming full-blown.

What Is SAD?

Explain that SAD is a form of clinical depression. Clinical depression involves experiencing at least five significant changes in mood and behavior that last most of the day, nearly everyday for 2 weeks or longer and cause distress and impairment in day-to-day life. The possible symptoms that can be present in SAD and in nonseasonal depression are the same. However, SAD is different from nonseasonal depression in that it tends to recur every year and follows a seasonal pattern of onset in the fall or winter and remission in the spring or summer. In contrast, nonseasonal depression can occur at any time, often in response to stressful life events.

Symptoms of SAD

Ask group members to look at their Identifying SAD Symptoms forms that they completed for homework. Tell them that you are going to talk about some of the symptoms of SAD and would like their input based on their own experiences. Use the following questions in your discussion:

- *How do you know when you or someone else is experiencing SAD?*

- *What are the things you notice or the signs/symptoms?*

List responses in four columns across the board *without* telling the group what the column headings are or what they mean. Separate responses into the following categories:

Physical: low energy, appetite changes (craving starches or sugars), increase in appetite, loss of appetite, weight gain or loss, muscle tension, pain, stomachache, headache, sensations of being weighted down or walking through water.

Emotional: depressed or anxious mood, sadness, feeling blue, decreased enjoyment or interest in things previously liked, irritable mood.

Cognitive: trouble concentrating, forgetfulness, thoughts about being worthless or a failure, negative thoughts about winter (e.g., "I can't cope with this," "I hate winter," and "Winter is never going to end"), thoughts about death or suicide.

Behavioral: less active, withdrawing from others, crying, sleep problems (oversleeping, napping, insomnia, or restless sleep), changes in eating (overeating, excessive carbohydrate consumption, or eating less).

Point out the diversity of symptoms and the polar opposites (e.g., increase in and loss of appetite). Explain that any two people with SAD can have very different symptoms. Now ask participants what each of the things listed in each unnamed category have in common. Have the group to try to name the titles of the columns and then add them to the board ("Physical," "Emotional," "Cognitive," and "Behavioral").

Degree of Emotional Symptoms

This section discusses the varying degree of symptoms, in particular, emotional symptoms. First, ask the group how they define emotions. Ask participants for examples of words that we use to describe to ourselves or to others how we are feeling. Put "I feel_____" on the board and have participants fill in the blank.

Discuss the concept of emotional continuity. Ask members whether our emotions are like an on–off light switch or more like a dimmer switch.

Explain that emotions are not all or nothing—they have various degrees. Choose one emotion from the list generated by the group and discuss how to use a 0–10 scale to describe its degree.

Next, explain the difference between sadness and depressed mood. It is normal for people to feel sad at times, especially in the face of loss or disappointment. The depressed mood associated with clinical depression is more intense (like the 7–10 level of sadness). In depression, the sad feelings are present most of the day, nearly every day for 2 weeks or longer, and can lessen self-esteem.

Tell the group that any one of the symptoms on our list from any column can be thought of on a continuum like this. We all have trouble sleeping or have low energy at times, but when these symptoms occur to a greater degree and last for 2 weeks or longer, they may be a sign of SAD.

The Vicious SAD Cycle (10 min)

Discuss how all the different types of SAD symptoms can interact or influence each other. The SAD cycle could start with any one of these symptoms. Use the following dialogue to illustrate this cycle:

For example, if you are feeling especially fatigued, you could end up sleeping too much. Your tiredness and oversleeping might make you feel less like doing things that you would normally enjoy or being around other people. This could then make you feel sad, which may actually make you have even less energy and want to sleep even more, etc.

Give other examples of the SAD cycle. Explain that the cycle is like a snowball effect in which SAD symptoms gradually increase. Inform the group that there is some research to suggest that SAD usually starts with one or two symptoms in the early fall and then gradually the other symptoms build on top of those. For many—but certainly not all—people with SAD, fatigue, oversleeping, and increased appetite come first. Ask group members these questions to help them think about their individual SAD cycles:

- *Have you ever noticed which SAD symptom starts your cycle?*

- *What symptoms follow along behind?*

- *What is your pattern of symptoms?*

Tell the group that the good news is that they can intervene on any one component to reverse the cycle. In this group, they will learn how to intervene at the cognitive and behavioral levels.

- Cognitive intervention—learn to view things in a less negative light

- Behavioral intervention—increase the number of pleasant activities

Prevalence of SAD (5 min)

Explain that, in general, SAD prevalence increases with latitude in the United States. We can think of SAD symptoms on a continuum in the general population. At Northern latitudes, the majority of people experience SAD symptoms to a certain extent and very few people do not experience any changes in their behavior during fall and winter. People who experience moderate changes with the seasons are said to have subsyndromal SAD or (S-SAD), also known as the winter blues. Population studies have found that the prevalence of SAD in U.S. adults ranges from 1.4% in Florida to over 9% in New Hampshire and Alaska (Booker & Hellekson, 1992; Rosen et al., 1990). S-SAD is even more common than SAD and ranges in prevalence from 2.6% in Florida to 19% in Alaska. The bottom line is that SAD symptoms are very common and get more common as distance from the equator increases.

Causes of SAD (15 min)

After more than two decades of research, we still do not know why people experience SAD. It is clear that winter or something about it is somehow related to SAD onset, but the specific mechanism is still not known for sure. Explain to the group that there are some hypotheses (or educated guesses), but none of these has been definitively proven.

Phase-Shift Hypothesis

Biological (circadian) rhythms of individuals experiencing SAD may be abnormally phase delayed (i.e., shifted later than normal) in response to shortened day length during the winter. These body rhythms are linked to the day–night cycle and operate on roughly a 24-hr clock. The body's biological clock (a tangle of neurons in the part of the brain called the hypothalamus) takes cues from light that enters the eyes and controls the release of hormones that influence alertness, hunger, and sleepiness. The level of one of these hormones, melatonin, rises in the evening to make us feel sleepy and then falls before dawn to help us wake up. The phase-shift hypothesis proposes that later dawns in the winter make the biological clocks of people with SAD run slow, meaning that their melatonin levels have not had enough time to fall by morning, and it is difficult to wake up because their biological clocks are still telling their bodies that it is night. These delays in body rhythms lead to feeling out-of-sync with the natural day–night cycle. This hypothesis likens SAD to jet lag that lasts for months.

Photoperiodic Hypothesis

According to this model, people with SAD may have retained a primitive biological mechanism for tracking changes in day length (and, therefore, changes in the seasons). This hypothesis likens people with SAD to photoperiodic mammals or mammals that are highly influenced by seasonal changes in the day–night cycle, such as sheep, cattle, and rodents. These animals' bodies use day length to determine what season it is, and in turn, determine the appropriate times to breed, hibernate, and forage for food. This hypothesis relates to the hormone melatonin mentioned previously, but is more focused on the overall length of the period of melatonin release than on how the circadian rhythm is affected based on the ebb and flow of melatonin. In humans, the pineal gland releases the hormone melatonin from dusk to dawn. Melatonin is commonly referred to as "the hormone of darkness" because the biological clock begins to signal its release in the late evening and its offset in the morning. In people with SAD, the photoperiodic hypothesis proposes that the period of melatonin release at night is longer in the winter than it is in the summer, whereas in people without SAD, how long the body is releasing melatonin each night does not differ across the seasons. A research study conducted by Thomas Wehr and colleagues at the National Institute of Mental Health found that SAD patients had a difference in the nighttime length of melatonin release in the winter versus summer of about 38 min, whereas there was no such difference in controls without SAD (Wehr et al., 2001). The summer–winter difference in nighttime melatonin release observed in SAD individuals may indicate that their bodies use day length to track the changing seasons and use this information to lengthen melatonin release in winter and shorten it in summer. Given that only people with SAD showed this seasonal change in nighttime melatonin release, it is possible that only people with SAD track the changing seasons biologically. This might be part of the reason why people with SAD feel and behave differently in the summer than they do in the winter. This hypothesis has not been tested again in another study so the jury is still out on whether or not lengthened melatonin release in winter is a cause of SAD or is rather just a consequence of having SAD.

Photon-Count Hypothesis

SAD may result when a dose of light (total number of photons received by the retina) falls below a critical threshold that is needed to maintain well-being. According to this model, any decrease in environmental lighting (e.g., cloudy weather) regardless of season should produce SAD symptoms.

Serotonin Hypothesis

Serotonin is a neurotransmitter (chemical messenger between neurons in the brain) that is involved in regulating sleep, appetite, and biological rhythms. In humans, levels of serotonin in the brain are lowest in the winter and highest in the summer. Scientists have shown this by examining the brains of people who died in different seasons (Carlsson, Svennerholm, & Winblad, 1980) and by examining blood samples drawn in different seasons from living people through a catheter in the internal jugular vein in the neck, which collects blood coming from the brain (Lambert, Reid, Kaye, Jennings, & Esler, 2002). Given that serotonin varies with the seasons and that SAD tends to be related to significant seasonal changes in sleep and appetite, there may be a role for serotonin in SAD symptom onset in the winter. However, it is not known exactly how low serotonin levels could lead to the symptoms of depression. It is possible that SAD-prone individuals may be especially sensitive to these seasonal changes in serotonin levels or may show an even larger wintertime decrease in serotonin than people without SAD. At the time of writing, there is no available test to measure brain serotonin levels in a living person. Because serotonin levels in the brains of people with SAD cannot be measured directly, this theory remains a hypothetical explanation for SAD.

Remind the group that all of these are just educated guesses; none of these hypotheses has been proven.

Psychological Factors in SAD (10 min)

Next, explain that even if biological factors are involved in SAD onset, psychological factors may be involved in maintaining SAD symptoms. We do not believe that SAD is a purely biological process or that people with SAD have to passively surrender to their biology and suffer from SAD symptoms every year. Instead, we believe that thoughts and behaviors also play a role in SAD and that these thoughts and behaviors are within a person's control and can be changed to reduce or eliminate SAD symptoms. Use the following example to illustrate:

> *For example, as the days get shorter, you may have certain expectations for what's ahead. You may think, "Oh no, it won't be long now. Here comes winter again. In no time, I'll be suffering from SAD." These thoughts may lead you to change your behavior by withdrawing from other people, spending more time on the couch or in bed, and doing less of the things you enjoy.*

Ask group members what they think about or say to themselves when they notice the leaves changing or when they are watching the weather report and see the minutes of sunshine decreasing every day. Ask group members how these thoughts influence the everyday things they do. Explain that negative expectations and becoming less active or engaged may actually influence SAD symptoms—make them start earlier, last longer, or be more intense.

Emphasize that group members can do something about the negative thinking style and reduced activity level that can make SAD worse:

> *Just because you are biologically prone to experience SAD does not mean that there isn't anything you can do about it. If you were biologically prone to heart disease, what steps would you take to try to prevent getting it? (Exercise, low-fat diet, reduce stress, quit smoking, etc.) Through CBT, you can change your thoughts and your behavior to begin to feel better. So, in other words, you don't have to be a victim of your body, which is telling you to retreat and hibernate the winter away!*

Tell the group that people with a more biological nonseasonal depression—depression that occurs out-of-the-blue, without any apparent life event triggering it—also tend to get better with CBT just like those who get depressed in reaction to life circumstances. CBT has shown to work just as well as medications for this biologically caused depression (which presumably results from a neurotransmitter imbalance and/or genetic factors). Regardless of the cause of depression, CBT treatment can help improve the depressive symptoms. It is good news that the treatment does not have to match the initial cause of the depression because that means there are several ways to intervene.

Homework (3 min)

✎ Have group members complete the Pleasant Activities Rating Scale.

✎ Have group members review Session 2 of the workbook.

✎ Have group members read the overview of Session 3.

Chapter 5

Session 3: How Activities Relate to Mood and Thoughts

(Corresponds to session 3 of the workbook)

Materials Needed

- Group members' completed Pleasant Activities Rating Scales

- 3 × 5 cards for positive self-statements

- Nametags

- Flip chart or writing board

- Copy of client workbook

Outline

- Set agenda (2 min)

- Review content of Session 2 (5 min)

- Review Pleasant Activities Rating Scale homework (20 min)

- Discuss pleasant activities and how they relate to mood and thoughts (25 min)

- Teach the group how to reverse the depressed mood–activity level cycle (5 min)

- Teach the group how to change thoughts in order to increase activity level (10 min)

- Help group members choose positive self-statements and plan a pleasant activity (20 min)

- Assign homework (3 min)

Setting the Agenda (2 min)

Begin the session by setting the agenda and writing it on the flip chart. Refer to the outline at the beginning of this chapter and add any other topics particular to the group.

Review of Session 2 (5 min)

Briefly review the following points from Session 2:

1. Common signs and symptoms of SAD (Ask the group whether anyone can name the main categories symptoms fall into—physical, emotional, cognitive, and behavioral. Ask the group to give a few examples of symptoms from each category.)

2. Interaction of SAD symptoms in a vicious cycle that may start with any one symptom

3. Prevalence of SAD

4. Possible causes of SAD: phase-shift, photoperiodism, photon-count, and serotonin hypotheses

5. Psychological factors that may be involved in onset and maintenance of SAD

6. Effectiveness of CBT

Homework Review: Pleasant Activities Rating Scale (20 min)

Examine group members' Pleasant Activities Rating Scales. Everyone in the group should have been able to identify some activities they like doing. If not, tell participants that if they do not like to do anything currently, to think about things they typically enjoy doing during spring and summer. Get some examples from the group.

Discuss group members' reactions to completing the scale. Ask whether the group members learned anything about themselves by thinking about activities that they enjoyed. Maybe they realized how inactive they have become. Perhaps they forgot about some things they used to really enjoy, including some that can be done in the winter. Perhaps they realized that many of the activities they enjoy are summer specific.

Pleasant Activities (25 min)

Discuss what constitutes a pleasant activity. Basically, it is something a person enjoys doing for fun. Thus, every person has different pleasant activities because of different interests. Use examples from the group to illustrate the personal nature of pleasant activities.

Ask group members how they typically feel during and after doing one of their pleasant activities. Explain that the frequency with which a person engages in pleasant activities impacts mood:

- A high frequency of pleasant activities is associated with satisfaction and happiness

- A low frequency of pleasant activities is associated with depressed mood

Emphasize that people feel good when they do a lot of things they enjoy. Ask participants what they have noticed about their activity levels across different seasons ("Does it change at all, say from summer to fall to winter to spring?"). During winter, people with SAD commonly do not engage in many pleasant activities. However, during spring and summer, they frequently engage in pleasant activities. You may want to use the following dialogue in your discussion.

> *Your lack of activity in the winter is like cabin fever. This actually happens to a lot of people during winter, not just those with SAD. The winter season can make it difficult to be active in general. With SAD it's more extreme than that. People with SAD typically have little energy and their bodies seem to be telling them to sleep, sleep, sleep. This is like going into hibernation mode and leads to a lot of sleeping and sitting around versus doing a pleasant activity. In spring and summer, though, people with SAD become more active again.*

How Activities Relate to Mood

We do not think that the seasonal pattern in pleasant activities associated with SAD is just a coincidence. Instead, we think that the decrease in activity in the fall and winter is actually an important part of the problem in SAD and helps to maintain SAD symptoms. When a person is experiencing depressed mood with a SAD episode, she is less motivated to do things. This results in a decrease in pleasant activities. Use the following dialogue and show Figure 5.1 to illustrate this relationship.

> *When you feel depressed, you engage in fewer activities, which makes you feel even more depressed. More depressed, you then do even less, which intensifies your depression and so on the cycle goes.*

Explain that decreased activity may be a cause or a consequence of depressed mood (Use the metaphor of what comes first—the chicken

Depressed Mood  Do Less Activities

Depressed Mood
Intensifies

 Do Even Less
Things You Enjoy

Figure 5.1

The Negative Mood–Activity Level Cycle

or the egg). When a person's rate of pleasant activities is low, she is likely to experience depressed mood. Refer again to Figure 5.1 and use the following dialogue:

> *If for some reason or another, you are not able to be as active as usual, you may begin to feel depressed. Then feeling depressed, you may engage in even fewer activities. As you become less active, you feel even more depressed and so on the cycle goes.*

How Activities Relate to Thoughts

Lack of activity not only affects mood, but also tends to result in pessimistic thinking, which can bring mood down even more. Use the following dialogue to stimulate a group discussion:

> *When you are experiencing a lot of SAD symptoms and sitting around thinking about how bad and tired you feel (instead of doing a pleasant activity), how do you feel about yourself? What is your self-esteem like at these times? Do you feel worthless? Are you optimistic or pessimistic as you think about your life, your work, and future? Are you cursing the winter weather?*

Explain to the group that thoughts of worthlessness, pessimism, and blaming yourself for your own inactivity and fatigue are common among people experiencing SAD and are part of the negative mood–activity level cycle. Give examples ("I'm so useless I can't even get off the couch and do something.") and ask the group whether these kinds of thoughts are familiar.

Reversing the Depressed Mood–Activity Level Cycle (5 min)

A positive spiral of mood and activity is also possible. Show Figure 5.2 to illustrate the positive mood–activity level cycle.

Explain that people try to intervene on the emotional component first, but that is the hardest to change. It is not easy to just feel better, snap out of a sad mood, etc. It is less difficult to intervene at the behavioral level. Changes in behavior can lead to changes in emotions. Increasing the

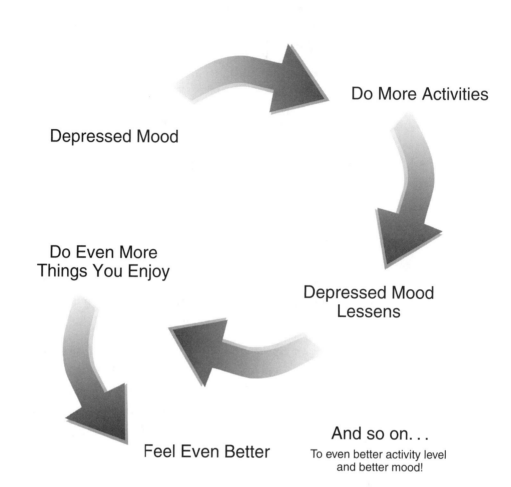

Do More Activities

Depressed Mood

Do Even More
Things You Enjoy

Depressed Mood
Lessens

Feel Even Better

And so on. . .
To even better activity level
and better mood!

Figure 5.2
The Positive Mood–Activity Level Cycle

number of pleasant activities is one way to intervene. Use the following dialogue to encourage participants to become more active:

> *To start a positive cycle, you have to get back in touch with your pleasant activities even though you may not feel like it. This is going to be really hard when you are experiencing SAD. You need to fight your cabin fever and low energy level to do something active. This is your chance to try to reverse the vicious SAD cycle so you have to commit to the challenge. You may need to really push yourself to engage in pleasant activities. You may not feel like doing anything at first. If you push yourself and do something active, I think you'll find you feel a little bit better though and have a little bit more energy. This will, in*

turn, make you feel like you can do a little more, which will make you feel a little better and so on.

Changing Thoughts to Increase Activity Level (10 min)

People with SAD often have negative thoughts that make them feel worse. These kinds of thoughts may keep them from trying the activities that just might make them feel better. Ask participants:

- *What are some unhelpful thoughts that get in the way of doing pleasant activities?*

- *What goes through your mind when you are contemplating doing something active?*

Elicit examples: "I can't do anything." "I'm so tired." "I just want to sleep." "I don't feel like it." "Things are too difficult." "I won't enjoy it anyway." "What's the point?"

Discuss how these thoughts impact the decision about whether to do a pleasant activity or whether to remain inactive. Emphasize the short- and long-term consequences of doing versus not doing a pleasant activity. In the short term, it may be easier not to do it, but in the long term being inactive helps to maintain the vicious SAD cycle of symptoms. In the short term it may take some effort to do it, but one may actually feel better during and immediately after doing the activity, and, in the long term, one will feel the benefits of the positive mood–activity level cycle if one regularly engages in pleasant activities. To increase the likelihood of doing pleasant activities, a person needs to replace negative thoughts with more positive ones. Ask participants:

- *When you catch yourself having these unhelpful thoughts, what else could you say to yourself to increase the chances of your doing a pleasant activity after all?*

Elicit examples: "I can do it." "I'll feel better if I do it." "Even if I'm not overjoyed by it, it beats sitting on the couch." "I know that, over time, the more pleasant activities I do, the better I will feel." "I do feel bad right now, but I have the power to change that somewhat by being active."

Have group members turn to the Positive Self-Statement Cards sheet in the workbook. Distribute 3 × 5 cards. On their cards have them write down statements that seem helpful to them and that they believe. They should keep these cards somewhere easily accessible (e.g., on the bathroom mirror or on the refrigerator).

They will be using these cards to help motivate themselves to do a pleasant activity of their choice in the coming week. Help participants select and plan a pleasant activity that is feasible to do, problem solve around any obstacles in doing the activity, and consider selecting a backup activity in the event that the first choice falls through. Keep it simple for now, choosing something that represents a modest increase in activity level with a minimum duration of 10 min. Have each member make a verbal commitment to the group to do a specific pleasant activity between now and next session. Ask each member:

- *What have you decided on?*

- *How will you make sure you get to do the activity?*

Tell participants that they should be prepared to tell the group about how their pleasant activity went and how they felt afterward. If they want, they may choose to involve a friend, family member, or significant other in the activity to help them get started this first time.

Homework (3 min)

✎ Have group members choose and complete a pleasant activity from the Pleasant Activities Rating Scale before next session.

✎ Have group members use the Positive Self-Statement Cards for motivation to complete activities.

✎ Have group members review Session 3 of the workbook.

✎ Have group members read the overview of Session 4.

Chapter 6 | *Session 4: Doing More to Feel Better*

(Corresponds to session 4 of the workbook)

Materials Needed

- Menu of Pleasant Activities

- Weekly Pleasant Activities Plan (additional copies of form optional)

- Nametags

- Flip chart or writing board

- Copy of client workbook

Outline

- Set agenda (2 min)

- Review content of Session 3 (3 min)

- Review pleasant activities completed for homework (20 min)

- Discuss important mood-related activities (5 min)

- Review possible problems in doing pleasant activities (10 min)

- Discuss how to get started on a balanced activity plan (8 min)

- Review strategies for creating balance (10 min)

- Introduce steps to activity scheduling (10 min)

- Have group members create an activity plan (20 min)

- Assign homework (2 min)

Setting the Agenda (2 min)

Begin the session by setting the agenda and writing it on the flip chart. Refer to the outline at the beginning of this chapter and add any other topics particular to the group.

Review of Session 3 (3 min)

Briefly review the following points from Session 3:

1. A high frequency of pleasant activities is associated with satisfaction and happiness; a low frequency of pleasant activities is associated with depressed mood.

2. During fall and winter, people with SAD tend to experience fatigue and lack of energy, like extreme "cabin fever," when they do not feel like doing anything.

3. Decreased activity may be a cause or a consequence of depressed mood (the chicken or the egg). There is a vicious cycle between decreased activity and depressed mood in which a person becomes increasingly depressed and less and less active over time.

4. By gradually increasing the number of pleasant activities, one can reverse this cycle to feel increasingly better over time.

5. People with SAD often have negative thoughts which make them feel worse and even less likely to engage in activities.

6. Positive self-statements can be used for motivation to follow through on activities.

Homework Review (20 min)

In the last session, you asked group members to select and complete a pleasant activity. Review what activities group members did. Discuss the emotional, cognitive, and physical impact of the activity for each group member:

- *How did you feel during the activity?*

- *How did you feel after the activity? How long did these feelings last?*

- *What did you think during the activity?*

- *What did you think after the activity?*

- *Did you notice any changes in your body or in your energy level?*

Ask whether group members used the Positive Self-Statement Cards to help motivate them to do the activity. Discuss whether these were helpful or whether they found other useful ways to motivate themselves.

Mood-Related Activities (5 min)

There is a subset of pleasant activities that is especially important in keeping mood positive. Elicit examples for each category from the group and discuss their impact on mood.

Positive social interactions—pleasurable interactions with other people (e.g., conversations or activities with friends or family).

Competency experiences—doing things that make you feel skilled and competent (e.g., performing a task well or learning to do something new).

Incompatible responses—doing things that are not compatible with feeling depressed (e.g., enjoying the company of a good friend, laughing or smiling, feeling truly relaxed, getting a good night's sleep).

Physical activities and exercise—doing as little as 10 min of continuous physical activity can improve mood. Engaging in regular, consistent aerobic exercise is even better (e.g., walking, swimming, biking, snow shoeing, or cross-country skiing). Current health guidelines recommend accumulating at least 30 min of physical activity (in 10 min bouts or more) over the course of most (at least 5) days a week (Pate et al., 1995).

Problems in Doing Pleasant Activities (10 min)

People with SAD may come across obstacles to doing pleasant activities. It is best to address these ahead of time so participants will know how to react to them when they occur. Go over the following common problems and discuss solutions.

Fatigue

Problem: People with SAD frequently find it difficult to engage in pleasant activities because they feel so tired. It is hard to motivate and get off the couch or out of bed to do something active.

Solution: *Push yourself to do it anyway and watch how the activity affects your mood. If it helps, you can remind yourself that activities make you feel a bit better, making yourself more likely to do activities in the future even if you are tired. Use positive self-statements to help with your motivation. Consider that if you do not do the pleasant activity, you will just stay stuck in the negative mood–activity level cycle and continue to feel tired.*

Problem: Sometimes people with SAD feel tired after doing a pleasant activity.

Solution: *Start with a small activity and gradually build up to bigger, longer ones so as not to tire yourself too much. Again, if you see over time that activities help your mood, you should look forward to doing them as a means to feel better. Your fatigue should even reduce over time as activities gradually improve your mood.*

Loss of Enjoyment or Pleasure in Activities

Problem: With SAD, like with depression, there is often a lack of pleasure in activities that are normally enjoyed. Recall that this is actually an emotional symptom and can increase or decrease in severity over time.

Solution: *Fake it until you make it. Studies show that the sense of enjoyment/pleasure comes back gradually with repetition of pleasant activities over time.*

Pressure From Necessary Activities That are Neutral or Unpleasant

Problem: Responsibilities such as work and household duties can often get in the way of doing fun things.

Solution: *Use time management to complete your responsibilities, but also schedule time for pleasant activities. Pleasant activities should not be the first thing to go when your schedule is tight, but instead should be a priority, especially now when you are actively working on ways to feel better. Also, you will be more likely to perform your responsibilities well if your mood has been boosted with pleasant activities.*

Lack of Care in Selecting Activities

Problem: Not selecting activities carefully can result in a mismatch between what one is actually doing and what one likes to do (e.g., spending the weekend working around the house instead of going shopping or to a movie).

Solution: *Think about the things you like to do and make time for them. Avoid scheduling "pleasant activities" that are really not at all pleasant for you.*

Change in the Availability of a Pleasant Activity

Problem: Sometimes something happens that removes the possibility of doing something one enjoys (e.g., death of a loved one, moving, end of a relationship, or getting a divorce). With SAD, sometimes activities that one likes doing in the spring or summer are less available or not at all available during winter (e.g., spending time outside, going to the beach, or gardening outdoors).

Solution: *Work on finding substitute pleasant activities or activity partners. You may be able to modify a summer-specific activity so it can be done in the winter (e.g., grow a window herb garden or dress warmly and continue to go for walks outside). Develop a new "wintertime interest" that* *you can look forward to this time of year (e.g., interest yourself in winter sports such as skiing, snow shoeing, or ice skating or in an indoor hobby that you would not ordinarily do in the spring or summer, such as artwork, home decorating, or crafting).*

Emotional Interference

Problem: Emotions such as anxiety, irritability, and discomfort can interfere with one's enjoyment of otherwise pleasant activities (e.g., being nervous or irritable in social situations makes it difficult to enjoy them).

Solution: *Identify the source of the emotional discomfort and work on removing it. If you feel irritable or anxious, find effective ways to relax before doing a pleasant activity. If certain pleasant activities make you feel anxious, regularly practice doing those activities; do not let yourself back out or make excuses, and you should become more and more comfortable doing them over time.*

Getting Started on a Balanced Activity Plan (8 min)

Tell group members what is required of them to increase their frequency of pleasant activities in order to improve their mood. Stress that they must commit themselves to putting the plan into effect. They must be willing to make choices, establish priorities, and rearrange their lives a bit.

Explain that the goal is to achieve a balance between the things they have to do and the things they want to do. It will involve planning, and they should try to anticipate any problems that might interfere with carrying out their plans. Emphasize that they will achieve a sense of self-control to the extent that they stick to their plans. By controlling their time, they are taking a step toward controlling their lives and their moods.

Creating a Balanced Activity Level

Tell the group that in making a plan, it is important to create a balance between:

(1) *Neutral or unpleasant activities*—things you have to do (e.g., housework, work, or errands)

(2) *Pleasant activities*—things you enjoy doing

Use the following dialogue for further explanation:

Balance between these kinds of activities allows you to accomplish the neutral and unpleasant things you have to do, while ensuring that you set aside time to also do the things you enjoy. It also ensures that you have some energy left over to do pleasant activities.

Also explain that the difference between these activities is very individual. What someone considers a chore, someone else may consider a pleasant activity (e.g., cooking or shopping).

Strategies for Balance (10 min)

Review the following strategies for creating balance. Prompt for examples and elicit additional strategies from the group.

Use Your Time Efficiently

1. Set aside blocks of time for neutral or unpleasant activities.

2. Create a "to do" list.

3. Consider whether those things really need to get done today.

4. Ask other people to help in getting necessary activities done.

5. Use a timer to stick to the amount of time designated for a neutral or unpleasant activity or for a pleasant activity.

Plan Ahead

1. Schedule each pleasant activity at least 1 day in advance.

2. Designate a time and place for each pleasant activity.

3. Do not allow yourself to make excuses or back out.

Anticipate and Prevent Problems

1. Avoid distractions and focus only on the pleasant activity at hand (e.g., unplug the phone).

2. Make the necessary arrangements ahead of time (e.g., make reservations, buy tickets, get supplies, or arrange for a babysitter).

3. Be prepared to substitute activities when unexpected problems arise. Have a backup plan if your planned activity involves another person who cancels or is dependent on getting outside and the weather suddenly becomes inclement. Otherwise, you will be at risk of not doing something pleasant and backsliding.

Steps to Activity Scheduling (10 min)

Next, teach the group the steps to activity scheduling: (1) set a specific goal; (2) plan, schedule, and record; and (3) reward yourself.

Step 1: Set a Specific Goal

Tell group members to consider what they are doing currently and decide what would be a modest increase in activity. They should make sure that the goal is reasonable and attainable. Remind them that the negative mood–activity level cycle came on gradually over time; reversing it will also be a gradual process that will take some time. They should select activities that are potentially pleasant for them, but also readily available to them. They may even want to incorporate some local events, take a class, join a club, develop a new interest, or learn about something new. The leisure section of the newspaper is full of ideas.

Step 2: Plan, Schedule, and Record

Tell group members that they will be using a weekly planner to plan out their activity levels. This will involve making an appointment with themselves to do a specific activity at a specific time each day. They will also record whether or not they followed through and how enjoyable each activity was. Scheduling activities in advance increases the likelihood that group members will actually do a given activity and also makes it more likely that they will regularly engage in pleasant activities over time. Just playing it by ear or trying to come up with activities spontaneously is potentially dangerous because it can easily lead back into the negative mood–activity level cycle. They should certainly take advantage of spontaneous activities when they arise (e.g., a friend calls and wants to meet for coffee today), but always have something planned in advance as well.

Step 3: Reward Yourself

Encourage group members to use small daily rewards and/or larger rewards for being active all week. Rewards may include other pleasant activities such as calling a good friend, eating out, making a small purchase, or seeing a movie.

Weekly Pleasant Activities Plan (20 min)

Next, have group members come up with a specific plan to increase their activity levels. First, have group members discuss what would be a reasonable activity level goal (i.e., desired number of activities per week and amount of time in activities) for now given their current activity levels. The minimum goal should be to do at least one pleasant activity per day for a minimum of 10 min everyday. Have group members share their specific goals with each other to make a public commitment to the group for increased activity level.

Second, have them fill out the Menu of Pleasant Activities form. They should use the Pleasant Activities Rating Scale to select target activities and include some activities that they currently do rarely or not at all, but are highly enjoyable. Then ask them to schedule an appointment with themselves to do some of these activities using the Weekly Pleasant Activities Plan. It is generally helpful to have them plan out activities for the next few days in session to get them started. Have the group members share their plans for the next few days.

Explain that each day's planned activity should be scheduled at least 1 day in advance and should be set for a specific time of day. They should record their activity appointments and follow through and rate their degree of enjoyment in the activity on the Weekly Pleasant Activities Plan.

Give the group the following general tips (see sample dialogues):

■ Make a habit of scheduling activities ahead of time

It's a good idea to make a habit out of planning pleasant activities in advance; for example, keeping the weekly schedule in a designated place and planning out the next day's pleasant activity each night at a specific time. If you make a ritual out of planning activities, you will be more likely to do it.

■ Choose activities that are relatively easy to do

Taking a vacation may be enjoyable, but not feasible at the moment. In the future, you may wish to add some long-range activity goals to work up to. For now, however, keep it simple. What activities could you realistically do this week?

Homework (2 min)

✎ Have group members finish developing their Menu of Pleasant Activities.

✎ Have group members schedule and complete at least one pleasant activity every day for at least 10 min per activity. They should record activity appointments, follow-through, and enjoyment ratings on the Weekly Pleasant Activities Plan.

✎ Have group members review Session 4 of the workbook.

✎ Have group members read the overview of Session 5.

Chapter 7

Session 5: What You Think Influences How You Feel

(Corresponds to session 5 of the workbook)

Materials Needed

- Thought Diary—4 Column (additional copies of form optional)
- Nametags
- Flip chart or writing board
- Copy of client workbook

Outline

- Set agenda (2 min)
- Review content of Sessions 3 and 4 (5 min)
- Review homework (20 min)
- Discuss the relationship between thoughts and mood (10 min)
- Present the A-B-C model (10 min)
- Review events that may cause negative thinking (10 min)
- Introduce the concept of automatic thoughts (10 min)
- Teach group members how to use a thought diary (20 min)
- Assign homework (3 min)

Setting the Agenda (2 min)

Begin the session by setting the agenda and writing it on the flip chart. Refer to the outline at the beginning of this chapter and add any other topics particular to the group.

Review of Sessions 3 and 4 (5 min)

Briefly review content from Sessions 3 and 4:

1. Categories of SAD symptoms: physical, emotional, cognitive, and behavioral

2. The negative mood–activity level cycle

3. The positive mood–activity level cycle

4. Mood-related activities

5. Possible problems in doing pleasant activities

6. Importance of balancing unpleasant or neutral activities with pleasant ones

7. Activity scheduling as a means of increasing pleasant activities

Homework Review (20 min)

Review group members' Weekly Pleasant Activities Plans. Ask for reactions to this assignment using the following questions:

■ *What was it like to do an activity for 10 min per day or more?*

■ *Did you enjoy the activities you practiced?*

■ *What was your mood like during and after doing the activity?*

■ *Any problems with finding time to do activities?*

■ *Did you have difficulty creating balance with responsibilities?*

If group members did not enjoy the activities they chose, they could modify their lists to include more enjoyable activities. If, however, their

SAD symptoms include loss of pleasure, they need to just go through the motions of doing activities; the sense of enjoyment in activities will come back eventually. Emphasize that activity planning is an important skill for participants to master in order to reverse the negative mood–activity level cycle. Encourage group members to stick with it. In the next week, they should try increasing the amount of time spent on pleasant activities.

Relationship Between Thoughts and Mood (10 min)

This session focuses on the cognitive symptoms of SAD. Tell the group that "cognitive" refers to thinking and explain that what we think can affect how we feel. Ask participants what they might be thinking and feeling in each of the following situations. (Note: If you get similar responses, ask for different types of thoughts and feelings that someone else might experience in these situations.)

Situation 1: *You are standing in a slow-moving line at the bank.*

Situation 2: *You are stuck in a traffic jam.*

Note how different people have different thoughts in reaction to the same situation and, therefore, feel different emotions as a result:

> *Frustrating or unpleasant things happen to everyone, but not everyone feels negative emotions in reaction to them. How can this be? Something comes between the event that is happening and what the person feels. That something is what the person is thinking (what he says to himself). Situations do not directly cause emotions. Instead, a person's thoughts directly contribute to the emotions he feels in specific situations.*

The A-B-C Model (10 min)

Present the A-B-C model (Figure 7.1) to the group.

Explain that "antecedent" means coming before; in this model the event comes before our thoughts and feelings. Use the following example to illustrate the model:

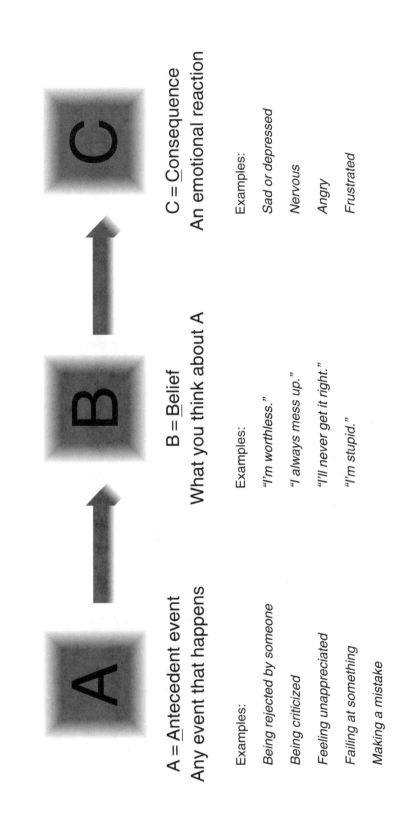

A = <u>A</u>ntecedent event
Any event that happens

Examples:

Being rejected by someone

Being criticized

Feeling unappreciated

Failing at something

Making a mistake

B = <u>B</u>elief
What you think about A

Examples:

"I'm worthless."

"I always mess up."

"I'll never get it right."

"I'm stupid."

C = <u>C</u>onsequence
An emotional reaction

Examples:

Sad or depressed

Nervous

Angry

Frustrated

Figure 7.1
The A-B-C Model

George and Bill are both on the dating scene. Both men ask the object of their affection out on a date and get shot down. George thinks to himself, "I'll never get a date again. I'm going to be single for the rest of my life. I'm a total failure at love and sure to be unloved forever." Bill says to himself, "Well, this is disappointing. I really liked this person, but I guess we weren't meant to be. If I continue to be myself, I'm bound to find someone I can have fun with."

Write this out on the board in the A-B-C format as you discuss. Ask the group how they think George and Bill would feel after this experience. Prompt for the answer that George's thoughts are likely to lead to depressed feelings. Bill, on the other hand, might feel appropriately sad and disappointed, but he would not be overwhelmed by his emotions.

Then ask the group, based on George and Bill's thoughts and feelings, how this experience might affect George's and Bill's behavior. That is, how are they likely to act toward dating in the future? Prompt for the answer that Bill is more likely to take constructive action (e.g., keep on searching for a dating partner) whereas George is more likely to give up.

Negative Thinking (10 min)

Review some events that might put someone at risk for negative thinking at the B (Belief) stage:

- Getting rejected by someone

- Being criticized or disapproved of

- Feeling under-appreciated

- Doing more than one's share of work without receiving credit

- Performing poorly, failing, or making a mistake

These things are all objectively negative or unpleasant types of events. However, explain that after a person gets in the habit of negative thinking, she may also start to see events that are not really all that bad in a negative light.

For example, you are at the store and you see a friend. You wave, but the friend does not wave back. If you are already in the swing of

negative thinking, you are likely to have negative thoughts such as,
"He doesn't like me. He is trying to avoid me because I'm miserable
with my SAD," leading to negative emotions such as sadness. However,
there are alternative, less negative interpretations of what happened.
For example, it could really be that the friend was distracted and did
not even see you.

Session 6 will introduce different types of negative thinking and their effects in more detail.

Automatic Thoughts (10 min)

Explain the thoughts or things we say to ourselves at stage B are called automatic thoughts. These thoughts are called "automatic" because they happen very quickly; they are an automatic "knee jerk" response to things that happen. They pop up spontaneously. We do not deliberately try to think them, and they are not the result of reasoning or logic. Occasionally, automatic thoughts are not preceded by an actual event or situation, but rather by a stream of thoughts, a daydream, or just thinking about events from the past.

Tell the group that everyone has automatic thoughts. Most of the time, we are barely aware of our automatic thoughts because they tend to be very brief. Usually, we are just aware of the emotion that follows the thought rather than the thought itself. That is, we recognize feeling sad, embarrassed, angry, anxious, or irritated, but do not tie these feelings to a thought. You may want to use an example to illustrate:

For example, as you sit here listening, if you think to yourself, "I am
such a dope. I don't really understand what the therapists are saying,"
you may feel frustrated or sad. If you think, "This cognitive-behavioral
therapy is too simple and will never work. It does not apply to me. The
problem is not with my thinking and behavior. I just need more light
to feel better," you may feel frustrated. In contrast, if you say to yourself,
"What the therapists are saying is really making sense. I think my SAD
could be helped by cognitive-behavioral therapy," you may feel hopeful
and more positive. You may or may not be aware of the automatic
thoughts, but you are probably aware of the emotions you feel.

Inform group members that with training, however, they can learn to become more aware of their automatic thoughts and how they are related to their feelings.

Explain that automatic thoughts can be either negative or positive. In individuals with SAD, automatic thoughts are frequently negative during the winter, contributing to a sad mood and maintenance of SAD symptoms. In the summer time, when people with SAD feel best, their automatic thoughts tend to be more positive, helping them to feel more satisfied and happier. We do not believe that it is simply a coincidence that people with SAD have more negative automatic thoughts in the winter, when they happen to feel their worst, and more positive automatic thoughts in the summer, when they happen to feel their best. Instead, we believe that the negative automatic thoughts are actually part of the problem, part of the SAD cycle that keeps them down in the winter, and that the positive automatic thoughts are part of the reason why they feel good in the summer.

Using a Thought Diary (20 min)

Elicit examples from the group and write them out on the board using the Thought Diary format (see Figure 7.2 for an example).

Date	Situation	Automatic Thought(s)	Emotion(s)
	Briefly describe situation (antecedent event), stream of thoughts, daydream, or image.	1) Write the automatic thoughts that accompany the emotions. 2) Rate belief in automatic thought (0–100%).	1) Specify sad, anxious, angry, etc. 2) Rate degree of emotion (0–100%).
1/24	I was looking over a report I submitted to my boss and found a typo.	I am such a dope. (90%) I messed up again. (90%) He will think I am careless and not a good worker. (80%) I should do a better job. (95%)	Sad (95%) Frustrated (85%)

Figure 7.2

Example of Completed Thought Diary—4 Column

Go through the following steps with the group:

1.   *Can you think of some time this past week when you felt sad, down, or upset in some way? What was happening then?*

2.   *What was going through your mind? While this was happening, how much did you believe that thought from 0 (not at all) to 100% (completely, totally believed it to be true)?*

3.   *What else went through your mind? How much did you believe it (0–100%)?* (Make sure to get all the thoughts. Don't stop with just one.)

4.   *After these thoughts, how did you feel? Sad, anxious, angry? How much did you feel that way? Give each emotion a rating from 0 (not at all) to 100% (the most intense I have ever felt this).*

Ask the group member whether she can see how what she was thinking influenced how she felt. Also inquire what she thinks would happen to her emotions if she discovered that her automatic thoughts were not true or at least not as true as she initially believed they were.

If a group member cannot think of any automatic thoughts, ask:

■   *What do you guess you were thinking about?*

■   *Do you think you could have been thinking about* (provide plausible possibilities)?

■   *What did this situation mean to you?*

■   *Were you thinking* (provide a thought opposite to the expected response)?

You can also ask the other group members for some possibilities of automatic thoughts in that situation.

If a group member cannot identify a problem situation, ask about general areas that have been on her mind (e.g., school, relationships, or work) and which situations bother her most.

You can ask how eliminating each area one-by-one would affect her feelings. You might also have the group member use imagery. Ask her to close her eyes and talk about any images that come to mind. Have her identify what thoughts occur when she visualizes an image.

Homework (3 min)

✎ Have group members continue scheduling activities using the Weekly Pleasant Activities Plan and modify it as needed.

✎ Encourage group members to try to add some new pleasant activities to challenge themselves.

✎ Encourage group members to strive for increasing the time for a pleasant activity to more than 10 min per day.

✎ Have group members complete the Thought Diary—4 Column form on a daily basis.

✎ Have group members review Session 5 of the workbook.

✎ Have group members read the overview of Session 6.

Chapter 8 | *Session 6: Cognitive Distortions*

(Corresponds to session 6 of the workbook)

Materials Needed

- Thought Diary—5 Column (additional copies of form optional)

- Nametags

- Flip chart or writing board

- Copy of client workbook

Outline

- Set agenda (2 min)

- Review content of Session 5 (5 min)

- Review homework (40 min)

- Discuss SAD-specific automatic thoughts (10 min)

- Introduce cognitive distortions (15 min)

- Have group members practice identifying cognitive distortions (15 min)

- Assign homework (3 min)

Setting the Agenda (2 min)

Begin the session by setting the agenda and writing it on the flip chart. Refer to the outline at the beginning of this chapter and add any other topics particular to the group.

Review of Session 5 (5 min)

Briefly review the content of Session 5, which focused on how our thoughts influence our feelings.

1.   A-B-C model (ask "What do A, B, and C stand for?")

   A = antecedent event (any event that happens)
   B = belief (what you think about A)
   C = consequence (an emotional reaction)

2.   Automatic thoughts are rapid, brief, and spontaneous thoughts that happen at stage B.

3.   Everyone has automatic thoughts, but we are not always aware of them. At first, we may only notice how we feel.

4.   Automatic thoughts can be either positive or negative. When people experience SAD, their automatic thoughts tend to be more negative during winter, when they feel their worst, than during the summer, when they feel their best.

5.   Negative automatic thoughts tend to lead to blue mood and make SAD even worse.

Homework Review (40 min)

Weekly Pleasant Activities Plan

Use the following questions to discuss how group members are progressing:

- *How is your Weekly Pleasant Activities Plan going?*
- *What did you do this week?*
- *How did you feel after doing an activity?*
- *How enjoyable were your pleasant activities?*
- *Have you had to change anything about your plan to make it work better?*

> *■ Have you had any difficulties creating balance with responsibilities?*
>
> *■ Is it time to change anything about your plan to challenge yourself more—add new activities, eliminate some activities that are becoming more routine, increase your time in activities?*

Thought Diary

Instruct group members to take out their Thought Diaries completed for homework. Go around the room to get some examples of situations, automatic thoughts, and emotions. Write these examples on the board in A-B-C format. Ask group members the following:

> *■ Do you see how what you thought influenced how you felt in that situation?*
>
> *■ What do you think would have happened to your emotions if you discovered that your automatic thought was not correct or at least was not as accurate as you originally believed?*

If a group member did not complete any Thought Diary entries, ask the following:

> *■ Can you think of some time this past week when you felt some type of negative emotion?*
>
> *■ What emotion or emotions were you feeling then? Sad, anxious, angry?*
>
> *■ What was going through your mind?*

Have the group member write in the answers on a Thought Diary form as he speaks.

SAD-Specific Automatic Thoughts (10 min)

Discuss automatic thoughts that people with SAD tend to have about the winter season in general, environmental cues that the seasons are changing into fall and winter, weather (e.g., precipitation or cold temperatures), and lack of light (e.g., short days or cloud cover). Go over the following scenarios and elicit examples of automatic thoughts from the group. After each scenario, ask group members the following:

- *What thoughts would you have in this situation?*

- *How would you feel?*

- *Can you see how your thoughts relate to how you feel emotionally?*

You can ask group members to close their eyes and imagine the scenarios as vividly as possible.

Scenario 1:

Imagine that you are watching the local weather forecast and it shows that the sunrise is taking place a minute later every day and that the sunset is taking place a minute earlier every day.

Scenario 2:

Summer is drawing to a close with the arrival of September. You notice the leaves gradually changing from green to shades of yellow, red, and orange.

Scenario 3:

Imagine that you are just getting out of bed, you feel groggy and tired, and you look out the window. The sky is dark and overcast, and there is a dusting of snow on the ground. You can feel the cold air coming in through your window.

Cognitive Distortions (15 min)

Explain to the group that negative automatic thoughts at stage B tend to fall into certain categories. We call these thoughts cognitive distortions because they are distorted or extreme in their interpretation of reality. Once negative thinking is in effect, cognitive distortions help to keep thinking negative so that most things, even neutral or positive events, are interpreted in a negative light. It is like putting on dark glasses through which everything seems pretty bad. With those dark glasses on, negative thinking can become a magnifying glass that blows up a trivial mistake, small imperfection, or minor event into a really big deal that makes one upset. Negative thinking can also downplay or make excuses for positive things that happen so those things are not experienced as genuinely positive. These cognitive distortions occur in everyone to some extent, but people with SAD think this way more than those without SAD, especially during the winter. It is useful for participants to be familiar with the specific cognitive distortions so they can recognize when their thinking is unhelpful. Review the following definitions adapted from *Feeling Good: The New Mood Therapy* (Burns, 1999) and illustrated with SAD-specific examples. Pause after each description and elicit personal examples from the group.

All-or-Nothing Thinking (Black-and-White Thinking)

You think in black and white terms; there are no gray areas. This type of thinking is unrealistic because things are seldom all or nothing, all good or all bad.

Example: A woman with SAD thinks, "Winter is totally bad and summer is totally good." In reality, some days are better than others in summer and winter alike. Some winter days may be more enjoyable and associated with more cheer than some summer days.

Overgeneralization

You assume that a one-time negative occurrence will happen again and again. You use words such as "always" or "never" to make generalizations.

Example: A man with SAD may have a tough day when he is suffering from a lot of pretty severe symptoms (e.g., fatigue, depressed mood, oversleeping, overeating, and loss of interest in activities). He may say to himself, "Because this particular day was so bad for me, every day for the rest of winter until spring arrives will surely be this terrible."

Mental Filter

You focus exclusively on negative details and ignore anything positive. As a result of filtering out the positives, you see the entire situation as negative.

Example: A woman with SAD hears about possible snow for 1 day in the week's forecast. She thinks, "The weather for the whole week is shot."

Disqualifying the Positive

You turn positives into negatives by insisting they "don't count." This allows you to maintain your negative outlook despite positive experiences.

Example: A woman with SAD is at a cocktail party. She appears to be having a good time, smiling, talking, and laughing. Afterward, she tells herself that she was just faking this because she had to look like she was having fun or the host would be insulted. A man with SAD spends an afternoon with his buddies and has such a good time, he forgets about his SAD. Afterward, he thinks, "That was a fluke. It doesn't really count. I still have SAD."

Jumping to Conclusions

In the absence of solid evidence, you jump to a negative conclusion. There are two types of this: "mind reading" and the "fortune teller error."

Mind Reading

You assume that you know what someone else is thinking. You are so convinced that the person is having a negative reaction to you, you do not even take the time to confirm your guess.

Example: A woman with SAD is at a holiday party with her family. Her grandchildren interact very little with her and she thinks, "They don't want to talk with me because I am so miserable with my SAD." Actually, they are so distracted by their new toys that the children barely talk at all to anyone.

The Fortune Teller Error

You act as a fortune teller who predicts only the worst for you. You then treat your unrealistic prediction as if it were a proven fact.

Example: A man with SAD thinks, "I will suffer from SAD symptoms repeatedly every single fall and winter for the rest of my life."

Magnification (Catastrophizing) or Minimization

You magnify negative things, blowing their importance out of proportion. The outcome of an event appears catastrophic to you.

Example: A man with SAD thinks, "Winter is horrible! This cold, dark weather will never go away, and I'll feel badly forever."

You minimize positive things, shrinking down their significance. You make good experiences out to be smaller than they are.

Example: The sun shines brilliantly on a cold December day and a woman with SAD thinks, "What use is this? It'll just be dark and dreary again tomorrow."

Emotional Reasoning

You take your emotions as proof of the way things really are. You assume something is true because you feel it is.

Example: Someone with SAD thinks, "I feel overwhelmed and hopeless during winter, therefore my problems must be unsolvable."

"Should" Statements

You build your expectations with "shoulds," "musts," and "oughts." When you do not follow through, you feel guilty. When others disappoint you, you feel angry and resentful.

Example: A person with SAD thinks "I should be able to cope with the winter season."

Labeling and Mislabeling

You label yourself or someone else, rather than just identifying the behavior.

Example: A person with SAD thinks, "I'm a loser for sleeping so much."

You mislabel an event by using inaccurate and emotionally extreme language.

Example: A person with SAD sees gray skies and thinks, "The weather is the pits; it's impossible to do anything on a totally depressing day like this."

Personalization

You take responsibility for things that you do not have control over. You feel guilty because you assume a negative event is your fault.

Example: A man with SAD thinks, "There's something wrong with me. It's my fault I have SAD."

Practicing Identifying Cognitive Distortions (15 min)

Have the group practice identifying cognitive distortions in the following example:

Imagine that the weather forecast is predicting a major winter storm. You think, "This is going to be terrible! I can't stand winter! Winter is

the worst! I'll never be able to get out of the house." You feel sad and
angry.

Cognitive Distortions:

All-or-nothing thinking—"Winter is the worst!"

Overgeneralization—"I'll never be able to get out of the house."

Magnification—"This is going to be terrible!" "I can't stand winter!"

Fortune Teller Error—"This is going to be terrible!" "I'll never be able to get out of the house."

Notice how some automatic thoughts contain more than one cognitive distortion. Explain that many negative thoughts fit into more than one category because there is a lot of overlap between the cognitive distortions.

Personal Examples

Next, have group members try to classify their own automatic thoughts as specific distortions. You can return to the examples that were generated from the homework assignments.

Homework (3 min)

✎ Have group members continue with their Weekly Pleasant Activities Plans. Encourage them to add more pleasant activities and/or increase the time spent on activities.

✎ Have group members continue to keep Thought Diaries and try to record at least one example every day. They should also attempt to classify their thoughts as specific cognitive distortions using the Thought Diary—5 Column form.

✎ Have group members review Session 6 of the workbook.

✎ Have group members read the overview of Session 7.

Chapter 9

Session 7: Evaluating Your Automatic Thoughts

(Corresponds to session 7 of the workbook)

Materials Needed

- Automatic Thought Questioning Form (additional copies optional)
- Nametags
- Flip chart or writing board
- Copy of client workbook

Outline

- Set agenda (2 min)
- Review content of Session 6 (5 min)
- Review homework (30 min)
- Discuss how to evaluate thoughts (2 min)
- Introduce the Automatic Thought Questioning Form (8 min)
- Discuss examples of questioning thoughts (40 min)
- Assign homework (3 min)

Setting the Agenda (2 min)

Begin the session by setting the agenda and writing it on the flip chart. Refer to the outline at the beginning of this chapter and add any other topics particular to the group.

Review of Session 6 (5 min)

Briefly review the contents of Session 6:

1. The vicious SAD cycle: how the different symptoms of SAD interact with each other to keep a SAD episode going.

2. Four categories of SAD symptoms: physical, emotional, cognitive, and behavioral.

3. Use of pleasant activity scheduling to turn the negative mood–activity cycle into the positive mood–activity level cycle in which one does more and feels better.

4. Thoughts can affect how one feels emotionally: the A-B-C model.

5. Types of cognitive distortions.

Homework Review (30 min)

Weekly Pleasant Activities Plan

Ask how group members are doing with planning and carrying out pleasant activities and balancing them with responsibilities. Modify plans as needed. Encourage members to add more activities or increase the amount of time spent on activities.

Thought Diary

Check to see whether group members completed the "Situation," "Automatic Thought(s)," "Emotion(s)," and "Distortions" columns of the Thought Diary with at least one entry per day. Was everyone able to identify their thoughts? Ask for examples and diagram them on the board. Discuss any problems with recognizing cognitive distortions.

Evaluating Automatic Thoughts (2 min)

Tell the group that though our initial automatic thoughts occur spontaneously, we actually have some control over our subsequent thoughts and the impact of our thoughts on mood. Over the past week, group members have started to be more aware of their automatic thoughts. The next step is to learn how to question and evaluate these thoughts to examine how accurate and useful they are.

Explain to participants that for each automatic thought they have, they need to consider several things and ask themselves some questions. Introduce the Socratic method:

> *Have you ever heard of the famous Greek philosopher Socrates? Socrates had a style of asking a lot of questions to try and evaluate things his students said or thought about. This method of questioning and evaluating is, in Socrates' honor, named the "Socratic method."*

Automatic Thought Questioning Form (8 min)

Ask group members to identify an important and distressing automatic thought from their Thought Diaries that they would like to evaluate using the Socratic method. Refer to the Automatic Thought Questioning Form in the workbook. Present the following four steps. You may want to use the following metaphor to help explain the first step:

> *To start, imagine that you are both a witness for the defense and an attorney for the plaintiff at a trial. First you are the witness and your automatic thoughts are your "testimony." You want to present the evidence in support of your testimony in order to convince the jury what you say is valid. Then you step out of the witness role and act as the attorney doing a cross-examination of that testimony. In the cross-examination, you want to logically point out any evidence against that testimony.*

Four Steps to Questioning Automatic Thoughts

1. Review the evidence. Ask yourself:

    ■ What is the evidence *for* this thought?
    ■ What is the evidence *against* this thought?

2. Review possible outcomes. Ask yourself:

   - What is the worst thing that could happen? Could I survive it?
   - What is the best thing that could happen?
   - What realistically is most likely to happen?

3. Consider the impact of your automatic thought. Ask yourself:

   - What are the results of my belief in this automatic thought?
     - How do I feel and act in response to this automatic thought?
   - What could be the results of changing my thinking?
     - Would I feel any differently?
     - Would I do anything differently if I could change the thought?

4. Problem solve about the situation that brought on your negative thinking. Ask yourself:

   - What could I do about it? Brainstorm possible solutions and consider the pros and cons of all options.
   - What would I tell someone else to do? What if a friend of mine was faced with the same situation?

Examples of Questioning Thoughts (40 min)

George's Thoughts About Dating

Have the group recall the example of George and Bill from last week (the two guys who asked someone out and got shot down). George said, "I'll never get a date again. I'm going to be single for the rest of my life. I'm a total failure at love and sure to be unloved forever." Ask the group to name George's A, B, and C. Write them out on the board in diagrammatic form.

Use the questions listed on the Automatic Thought Questioning Form to help the group evaluate George's automatic thoughts.

Personal Examples

Return to the group members' selected automatic thoughts from their Thought Diary homework. As a group, go through the Automatic Thought Questioning Form. Have one group member ask the questions and another answer the questions about her automatic thought. You and other group members can jump in with follow-up questions to explore as much information as possible. Be sure that the group does this in a supportive, objective way to logically evaluate the evidence for and against the thoughts. Have group members take turns in asking and answering the questions. Talk about the questioning process with the group and allow everyone to share their experiences.

Look for opportunities to practice evaluating SAD-specific Thought Diary entries about the winter season, environmental cues that the seasons are changing, weather, and lack of light. The process of evaluating SAD-specific thoughts is the same as that of evaluating any negative automatic thought. In reviewing the evidence, individuals with SAD tend to have historical evidence in support of these kinds of thoughts (e.g., "Winter is always a hassle for me," "I hate winter," "I can't function when the sun is not shining"). However, similar to any negative automatic thought, these thoughts tend to be global and overly negative in tone and include cognitive distortions. Examining evidence against SAD-specific thoughts involves looking for any personal examples that counter the negative thought (e.g., "Have you ever had a day when you felt OK in the winter? If not, are some winter days better than others? What was happening then? What were you doing and thinking then?"). Point out that the person's behavior in response to the thought, and the thought itself, plays a role in resulting feelings (e.g., sitting on the couch under a blanket rather than going to the gym or calling a friend in reaction to SAD-specific thoughts contributes to feeling down, above and beyond the fact that is winter, dark out, snowing, etc.). Pay particular attention to any thoughts related to external locus of control (e.g., thoughts that the season, weather, day length, sunlight availability, etc. directly and unilaterally determine how one feels) and look for opportunities to suggest a role for internal locus of control (i.e., what one thinks and does in response to those environmental cues directly influences feelings). You can also use this as an opportunity to question the fairness of "feeling like the weather" in a knee-jerk response and to instill an aggressive stance in participants to exercise the internal control they have over those external influences to gain control over mood.

Homework (3 min)

✎ Have group members continue with their Weekly Pleasant Activities Plans.

✎ Have group members continue to keep Thought Diaries using the 5-column form.

✎ Have group members use the Automatic Thought Questioning Form to evaluate and question at least one important, distressing automatic thought.

✎ Have group members review Session 7 of the workbook.

✎ Have group members read the overview of Session 8.

Chapter 10 | *Session 8: Rational Responses*

(Corresponds to session 8 of the workbook)

Materials Needed

- Thought Diary—7 Column (additional copies of form optional)
- Nametags
- Flip chart or writing board
- Copy of client workbook

Outline

- Set agenda (2 min)
- Review content of Session 7 (5 min)
- Review homework (30 min)
- Teach how to generate rational responses (10 min)
- Discuss the importance of believing in one's rational response (5 min)
- Evaluate the impact of rational responses (5 min)
- Discuss examples of rational responses (30 min)
- Assign homework (3 min)

Setting the Agenda (2 min)

Begin the session by setting the agenda and writing it on the flip chart. Refer to the outline at the beginning of this chapter and add any other topics particular to the group.

Review of Session 7 (5 min)

Briefly review the content of Session 7, including using the Socratic method and the steps to evaluating thoughts:

1. Review the evidence.

2. Review possible outcomes.

3. Consider the impact of your automatic thought.

4. Problem solve about the situation that brought on your negative thinking.

Homework Review (30 min)

Weekly Pleasant Activities Plan

Discuss how group members are doing with planning and carrying out pleasant activities and balancing them with responsibilities. Modify plans as needed. Encourage members to add more activities or increase the amount of time spent on activities.

Thought Diary

Check the "Situation," "Automatic Thought(s)," "Emotion(s)," and "Distortions" columns on group members' Thought Diaries. Discuss examples and diagram them on the board.

Automatic Thought Questioning Form

Review group members' Automatic Thought Questioning Forms and discuss how they went about evaluating their negative automatic thoughts. Address any questions or difficulties.

Generating Rational Responses to Automatic Thoughts (10 min)

Now teach the group how to generate rational responses. Begin with the following statements:

After first identifying negative automatic thoughts that are important and distressing and then evaluating and questioning those automatic thoughts to examine how accurate and useful they are, the next step is to look for alternative explanations. This involves coming up with a new, more accurate and helpful thought to replace the original problematic automatic thought.

Explain that we are adding a D to the A-B-C model (see Figure 10.1).

D = Dispute

Explain that at stage D, we try to change our automatic thought to something more realistic and helpful by asking ourselves:

- *Is there any other way to view or to think about this situation?*

- *What would be a more accurate and realistic thought to have?*

- *What would be a more helpful thought to have?*

If we see words like the following in our automatic thoughts, we question them:

- "Should"—*Why should I?*

- "Terrible, awful, etc."—*Is it really that bad? What is the worst thing that could happen? Could I survive it?*

- "Always"—*Is it really always or just this time or some of the time?*

The end result of this questioning is a "rational response," a thought we generate to take the place of or substitute for our original automatic thought. Our rational response should be more realistic and more helpful than our original automatic thought. Tell the group that a rational response is like a rebuttal to an automatic thought.

Importance of Believing in the Rational Response (5 min)

Explain to the group that with rational responses we are not trying to come up with something that is rosy and overly positive. Rather we want

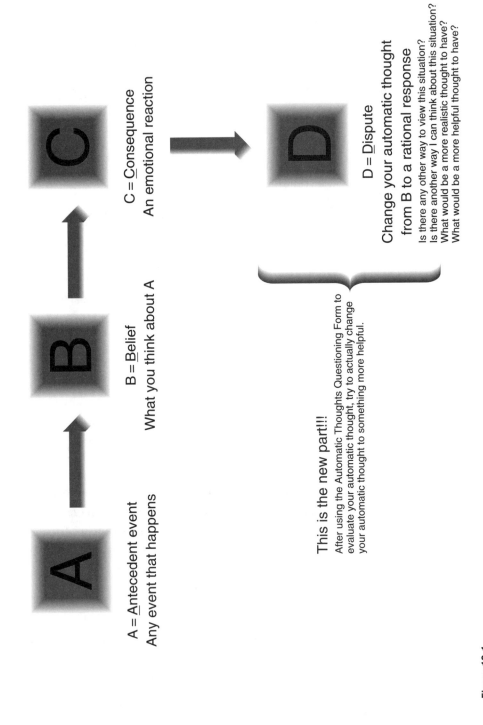

A = <u>A</u>ntecedent event
Any event that happens

B = <u>B</u>elief
What you think about A

C = <u>C</u>onsequence
An emotional reaction

This is the new part!!!

After using the Automatic Thoughts Questioning Form to evaluate your automatic thought, try to actually change your automatic thought to something more helpful.

D = <u>D</u>ispute

Change your automatic thought from B to a rational response

Is there any other way to view this situation?
Is there another way I can think about this situation?
What would be a more realistic thought to have?
What would be a more helpful thought to have?

Figure 10.1

The A-B-C-D Model

to substitute a thought that is more helpful, while still being realistic. Use the following examples to illustrate:

> *For example, if you have the thought, "I failed again," your rational response should not be "I always succeed at everything I do" because that is unrealistic: No one succeeds at everything they do 100% of the time. Instead, you should come up with something more realistic and less negative. For example, "I made a mistake this time, but I do most things well."*

Tell participants that the next step is to rate our belief in the new thought. After coming up with a rational response, we ask ourselves: "How much do we believe this rational response?"

Refer to the Thought Diary and explain how to use the 7-column form:

> *In the "Rational Response" column, you will write down what your rational response is under number 1 and how much you believe that rational response under number 2, where 0% is you don't believe it at all and 100% is you completely, totally believe it. Don't tell yourself something you don't believe. When you dispute your automatic thought, make sure you end up with statements you can accept. If you end up with a statement you don't have any faith in, keep on challenging your automatic thoughts until you arrive at a better rational response.*

Explain that the higher the belief rating for a given rational response, the more effective it will be in countering our original automatic thought. For each automatic thought, it is recommended that we generate several rational responses that we believe highly in order to have a strong, convincing rebuttal to our original automatic thought.

Evaluating the Impact of Rational Responses (5 min)

Tell the group that if we have generated a series of good, helpful rational responses, this process should reduce our belief in negative automatic thoughts and make us feel better. The next step is to evaluate the impact of our rational responses on our original automatic thought and on our emotions.

The impact on our original automatic thought is indicated in the last column of the Thought Diary. Under "Outcome," we re-rate our belief in the original automatic thought. In other words, now that we have challenged the automatic thought and generated a rational response, how much do we believe that automatic thought we had in the first place? 0% is we do not believe it at all, and 100% is we still totally, completely believe it. If we have generated a good, helpful rational response, our degree of belief in the original automatic thought should go down.

The impact on our emotions is also indicated in the "Outcome" column. Under number 2, we list any emotions we feel now. In other words, what was the impact of coming up with a rational response to our automatic thought on our emotional state? We may still have some of those same emotions we had in the original "Emotion(s)" column. However, they should now be less in degree. We may also experience new emotions after generating a rational response, maybe even some positive emotions such as hopefulness or happiness.

Use the following example to illustrate:

> *If you originally had the automatic thought "I failed again" and your rational response is "I made a mistake this time, but I do most things well," you should believe in that rational response and see a noticeable change in those original emotions. For example, if you first had the emotion of sadness rated 85% in the "Emotion(s)" column, after evaluating your automatic thought and coming up with a rational response, we would hope your sadness would be reduced, maybe to a degree of 35%.*

Examples of Rational Responses (30 min)

George's Rational Response

Have the group recall the example of George and Bill from last week (the two guys who asked someone out and got shot down). Review George's A, B, and C.

A = the person he asked out declined his invitation

B = "I'll never get a date again. I'm going to be single for the rest of my life. I'm a total failure at love and sure to be unloved forever."

C = felt depressed

Discuss with the group what George's "D" (rational response) could be: "How could he dispute each automatic thought at B to make his thinking more realistic and feel less down?" "What could he say to himself to view the original situation (A = being rejected by someone) in a less negative and more helpful light?" Give an example if needed:

> *Is it really that bad? No, I guess not. This is only one person in a huge sea of people that I could ask out. I'm sad at being turned down, but I doubt I'll really end up never getting a date again. In fact, chances are that I will date again. I'm not really a failure at love. I've had plenty of dates before. And I'm not unlovable. My family loves me.*

Personal Examples

Take another look at group members' Thought Diaries from the past few days. Ask them to try to generate rational responses to one of their automatic thoughts. Diagram out the "Situation," "Automatic Thought(s)," "Emotion(s)," "Distortions," "Rational Responses," and "Outcome" columns on the board. (Note: You can also return to the previously diagramed Thought Diary examples from the homework review at the beginning of this session.)

Help the group members to go through the questions that occur at D (listed on the A-B-C-D model) to come up with some appropriate rational responses. Write the rational responses, how much the group member believes each rational response, and the outcome (belief in original automatic thought and remaining emotions) on the board; also ask the group member to write these into his Thought Diary. During the exercise, ask each participant the following:

- *What rating would you give that rational response for amount of belief (i.e., belief in rational response from 0 to 100%)?*

- *What is the outcome for your belief in the original automatic thought (0–100%)?*

- *What emotions do you feel now and at what intensity (0–100%)?*

Note: You may not have time to review examples from every participant. The other group members should benefit vicariously from observing the process and can also participate in generating potential rational responses for the examples reviewed.

SAD-Specific Examples

Either in this session or in upcoming sessions, look for opportunities to practice generating rational responses to SAD-specific Thought Diary entries about the winter season, environmental cues that the seasons are changing, weather, and lack of light. Refer back to the contents of Session 7 for suggestions regarding evaluating SAD-specific thoughts. Draw from this evaluation process to generate possible rational responses. Look for ways to rephrase thoughts that reflect global negativism about winter (e.g., "I hate winter") into rational responses that are more helpful (e.g., "I prefer summer to winter"). Point out the impact on feelings and likely subsequent behavior in reaction to the original thought versus the rational responses.

Homework (3 min)

✎ Have group members continue with their Weekly Pleasant Activities Plans.

✎ Have group members keep Thought Diaries using the Thought Diary—7 Column form, which includes columns for rational responses and the outcome.

✎ Ask group members to try to look for patterns in their automatic thoughts as they complete the Thought Diaries.

✎ Have group members review Session 8 of the workbook.

✎ Have group members read the overview of Session 9.

Chapter 11 | *Session 9: Core Beliefs*

(Corresponds to session 9 of the workbook)

Materials Needed

- Nametags

- Flip chart or writing board

- Copy of client workbook

Outline

- Set agenda (2 min)

- Review content of Session 8 (5 min)

- Review homework (50 min)

- Introduce core beliefs (10 min)

- Discuss the difference between core beliefs and automatic thoughts (10 min)

- Have group practice identifying core beliefs (10 min)

- Assign homework (3 min)

Setting the Agenda (2 min)

Begin the session by setting the agenda and writing it on the flip chart. Refer to the outline at the beginning of this chapter and add any other topics particular to the group.

Review of Previous Sessions (5 min)

Briefly review the contents from previous sessions, beginning with the categories of symptoms: physical, emotional, cognitive, and behavioral. Remind the group that these areas all interact. Treatment of one will likely improve other areas as well.

So far, the group has learned techniques to help depression on two important levels:

- Behavioral—pleasant activity scheduling

- Cognitive—evaluating negative automatic thoughts and replacing them with rational responses

Homework Review (50 min)

Weekly Pleasant Activities Plan

Ask how group members are doing with planning and carrying out pleasant activities and balancing them with responsibilities. Modify plans as needed. Encourage members to add more activities or increase the amount of time spent on activities.

Thought Diary

Review all the columns of participants' Thought Diaries ("Situation," "Automatic Thought(s)," "Emotion(s)," "Distortions," "Rational Responses," and "Outcome"). Check that they have recorded at least one entry a day. Discuss how it went and problems, if any. Go around the room and get examples and diagram them on the board. Pay special attention to the rational responses and their impact (on emotions and belief in the original automatic thought). Suggest additional rational responses as needed. Emphasize any positive outcomes.

Introduction to Core Beliefs (10 min)

Explain that automatic thoughts are the words that actually go through our minds and are very close to our conscious awareness. This makes it possible to identify, evaluate, and question automatic thoughts and reframe them as rational responses in order to experience some relief. There is, however, a deeper, less conscious level to our thinking that influences what we think about, what we do, and how we feel. This deeper level of thinking is made up of our core beliefs. In this session and the next, the group will focus on core beliefs, in particular, what core beliefs are, how they develop, how to identify them, and how to change negative core beliefs to make them more helpful.

Defining Core Beliefs: How They Are Learned and Maintained

Discuss with the group how, during childhood, people learn certain ways of thinking about themselves, other people, and the world. This learning is important so we can make sense of things as we grow up. Core beliefs are our most central, fundamental, important beliefs. They are the things we wholeheartedly believe to be true about ourselves, other people, and the world in general. We consider our core beliefs as absolute truths or just "the way things are."

For most of our lives, our core beliefs tend to be positive (e.g., "I am likeable," "I am competent," "I am in control," "Other people are trustworthy," "The world is a good place," and so on).

When people feel depressed, their negative core beliefs tend to surface (e.g., "I am a failure," "I am unlovable," "Other people are critical," or "The world is a dangerous place"). During winter, when individuals with SAD are feeling their worst, we expect that their negative core beliefs are activated and wreak havoc on their thinking, helping to maintain the symptoms of SAD. During summer, when individuals with SAD are feeling their best, we expect that their positive core beliefs are activated, helping to contribute to good mood and sense of well-being. People with SAD may not believe their negative core beliefs in the spring or summer, when they are not feeling depressed. However, it is to be expected that they believe their negative core beliefs almost completely when they are feeling depressed in the winter. You may want to use the following dialogue in your discussion:

Once a negative core belief is activated (when you are feeling depressed), you easily notice any evidence that seems to support it, but ignore or discount any evidence that contradicts it. It's like having a screen around your head that allows anything that fits with the negative core belief through and stops anything that doesn't fit.

For example, a college student who is depressed may have the core belief, "I'm inadequate." He would, therefore, ignore that he got an A on a recent biology exam (maybe saying, "The test was easy"). Instead, he would pay special attention to getting a C on a calculus exam because this would confirm his negative core belief of inadequacy.

Core Beliefs Versus Automatic Thoughts (10 min)

Explain to the group that core beliefs are different from our automatic thoughts. Our core beliefs are not as close to our conscious awareness, but they certainly do affect our day-to-day and moment-to-moment automatic thoughts. Our core beliefs influence the way we view daily situations and, therefore, influence the way we think, feel, and behave. Core beliefs actually are what drive our automatic thoughts; they are like the root of our automatic thoughts. Core beliefs are the reason why different people have different automatic thoughts in reaction to the same situation.

Core beliefs fit into the A-B-C model as shown in Figure 11.1. Diagram this out on the board for the group. You can tell participants that the idea of core beliefs is a difficult concept to understand. To clarify, return to the example you've been using throughout this group (George and Bill are both on the dating scene. Both men ask the object of their affection out on a date and get shot down). Discuss what George's and Bill's core beliefs may possibly be or the way these men may generally think about themselves, other people, and the world. Give the following examples if needed.

George's Core Beliefs

Core beliefs about self—*I am unlovable. I am inadequate.*

Core beliefs about others—*Other people reject and hurt me. Other people remind me of my inadequacies.*

CORE BELIEFS
(Self, Others, World)

A = <u>A</u>ntecedent event
(Situation, stream of thoughts, or daydream)

B = <u>B</u>elief
(Automatic thoughts)

C = <u>C</u>onsequence
(Emotional reaction)

Figure 11.1
Core Beliefs and the A-B-C Model

Core beliefs about the world—*The world is a nasty place, full of opportunities for rejection.*

Bill's Core Beliefs

Core beliefs about self—*I am competent and worthwhile. I am lovable.*

Core beliefs about others—*Other people are generally good. Others accept me.*

Core beliefs about the world—*The world is a safe, accepting place where I can find happiness.*

Reiterate that core beliefs are the reason why different people have different automatic thoughts in reaction to the same situation. Emphasize that this higher level of thinking influenced the specific automatic thoughts that these men had in reaction to the same situation.

Identifying Core Beliefs (10 min)

In the last session, you asked participants to try to look for patterns in their automatic thoughts as they completed their Thought Diaries. Explain now that one way to identify our core beliefs is to look for themes in our automatic thoughts because, again, our core beliefs actually drive our automatic thoughts. Ask group members the following:

- *Do any of your automatic thoughts occur again and again?*

- *Does there seem to be any common theme among your automatic thoughts?*

- *Do your automatic thoughts suggest any ideas about how you think about yourself, other people, and the world?*

Note: Other ways to help participants identify core beliefs include (1) using the downward arrow technique to identify the underlying meaning associated with an important automatic thought that you hypothesize stems from a core belief (J. S. Beck, 1995) and (2) asking participants to complete a questionnaire that measures the extent to which a person has certain attitudes or core beliefs, such as the Dysfunctional Attitudes Scale (Weissman & Beck, 1978) or the Young Schema Questionnaire (J. Young & Brown, 2003).

Homework (3 min)

✎ Have group members continue with their Weekly Pleasant Activities Plans.

✎ Have group members continue to keep Thought Diaries using the 7-column form.

✎ Have group members keep looking for themes and patterns in their automatic thoughts so they can begin to learn what their core beliefs are.

✎ Have group members review Session 9 of the workbook.

✎ Have group members read the overview of Session 10.

Chapter 12 | *Session 10: Evaluating Your Core Beliefs*

(Corresponds to session 10 of the workbook)

Materials Needed

- Core Belief Worksheet (additional copies of form optional)
- Nametags
- Flip chart or writing board
- Copy of client workbook

Outline

- Set agenda (2 min)
- Review content of Session 9 (3 min)
- Review homework (40 min)
- Identify core beliefs (30 min)
- Discuss evaluating and changing core beliefs (3 min)
- Introduce the Core Belief Worksheet (10 min)
- Assign homework (2 min)

Setting the Agenda (2 min)

Begin the session by setting the agenda and writing it on the flip chart. Refer to the outline at the beginning of this chapter and add any other topics particular to the group.

Review of Session 9 (3 min)

Briefly review the content from Session 9:

1. Core beliefs are our most central, fundamental, important beliefs about ourselves, other people, and the world.

2. We consider our core beliefs as absolute truths or simply "the way things are."

3. We learn most of our core beliefs during childhood.

4. Core beliefs are different from automatic thoughts:

   o Automatic thoughts are the words that actually go through our minds and are very close to our conscious awareness.
   o Core beliefs happen at a deeper, less conscious level of thinking. They are at the root of our automatic thoughts.

Homework Review (40 min)

Weekly Pleasant Activities Plan

Discuss how group members are doing with planning and carrying out pleasant activities and balancing them with responsibilities. Modify plans as needed. Encourage members to add more activities or increase the amount of time spent on activities.

Thought Diary

Review all the columns of participants' Thought Diaries ("Situation," "Automatic Thought(s)," "Emotion(s)," "Distortions," "Rational Responses," and "Outcome"). Diagram examples on the board, paying particular attention to rational responses that were generated in response to automatic thoughts. Suggest alternative or additional rational responses as needed. Emphasize the positive impact of rational responses on belief in the original automatic thought and on emotions.

Identifying Core Beliefs (30 min)

Examining Automatic Thoughts

Reiterate that we can learn what our core beliefs are by examining our automatic thoughts for indications of how we generally think about ourselves, others, and the world. Ask participants whether they noticed any patterns or themes in their automatic thoughts suggestive of underlying core beliefs. Discuss group members' observations in reviewing their Thought Diaries. If a group member is struggling with this, consider using the downward arrow technique (J. S. Beck, 1995) to examine the meaning of an important, distressing automatic thought (e.g., Assuming that automatic thought is true, what would that mean to you or about you?).

Common Core Beliefs

Explain that core beliefs often fall into two broad categories: core beliefs surrounding themes of being helpless and core beliefs surrounding themes of being unlovable (J. S. Beck, 1995). Have group members give examples of these kinds of core beliefs.

Challenging and Changing Core Beliefs (3 min)

Now that participants have some ideas about what their core beliefs are, it is important to work on making any negative core beliefs they have more realistic and accurate, more helpful, and less negative and more positive in tone. You may want to use the following metaphor:

> *Think of your core beliefs as an iceberg. They are really important beliefs you have and wholeheartedly believe to be true. It's difficult to logically evaluate and eventually change them. However, by gradually chipping away at the iceberg, it is possible to change your core beliefs.*

Tell the group that the process of evaluating our core beliefs is similar to how we evaluated and questioned our automatic thoughts using the Socratic method. However, it is usually a lot more difficult to logically evaluate our core beliefs because they are a lot more important to us and we believe them more than our automatic thoughts. The process of replacing an unhelpful, negative core belief with a more helpful, positive core belief is somewhat similar to replacing a negative automatic thought with a rational response. Again, it is usually harder and more time consuming to replace core beliefs because they are more central and are more strongly believed by us than our automatic thoughts are.

Core Belief Worksheet (10 min)

Introduce the Core Belief Worksheet to the group. Say that it is an organized way of working on our core beliefs and is similar to a Thought Diary, but is made for core beliefs instead of automatic thoughts. The Core Belief Worksheet combines the steps of evaluating, questioning, and generating new, more helpful core beliefs.

Provide participants with copies of a blank Core Belief Worksheet. Have them refer to the completed example in their workbooks (same as Figure 12.1). Explain how they will be completing the form as part of this session's homework. At the top, they will write in a core belief that seems important, as determined from their Thought Diaries. They will write down how much they believe that core belief right now from 0 to 100%. Then they will think about that core belief in the past week and write down the least and most they have believed that core belief from 0 to 100% in the spaces provided in the worksheet. Refer to the completed example worksheet:

The core belief in the example is, "I am a failure." This depressed young woman believes that she is a failure 80% right now, but believed it as much as 90% and as little as 70% at some other times this past week.

Next, group members will look at the evidence for and against their core beliefs.

Core Belief	Strength (0–100%)	Evidence for with BUT statements	Evidence against	New Belief	Strength (0–100%)
I am a failure.	Current: 80%	Growing up, my mother often made statements comparing me to my sister, suggesting that I was not as good as my sister (not as smart, not as likeable, not as pretty, etc.) BUT that was only her opinion and today I understand that nurturing parents do not say such things to their kids.	I maintained excellent grades throughout my education and received lots of praise from my instructors.	I perform most things I do very well, but, like most people, I do not reach my top goal all of the time.	New Belief: 95%
	Most (past week): 90%	During my senior year of high school, I did not make a sports team that I really wanted to be part of BUT I did make this team every other year of high school and more students tried out at that year than ever before.	Most things I wrote under "evidence for" are specific times when I did not reach some top goal. I do reach my desired goal the vast majority of the time. Even when I do not reach my top goal, things work out for me and I do not end up as a total failure. I at least partially succeed.		Old Belief: 60%
	Least (past week): 70%	I did not get into the top college of my choice BUT that was a highly selective school and I ended up attending an excellent college. During college, I really struggled to pass my biology courses BUT many students struggled with biology and I earned high grades in all of my other courses.	I obtained a very good job that I perform well and continue to enjoy. Achieving things is not the only way to define success or failure—having good relationships is important, too. I have good relationships with my family and friends.		

Figure 12.1

Example of Completed Core Belief Worksheet

Note. Adapted from *Cognitive Therapy: Basics and Beyond*, by J. S. Beck, 1995, New York: The Guilford Press.

On the left-hand side of the worksheet, they should list any evidence that supports the core belief. After they list something, instruct them to add a "BUT" statement with one or more other explanations for why that might have occurred (other than the core belief being true). Refer again to the example on the worksheet:

> *This young woman thought through her life and recorded specific events when she strongly held the belief, "I am a failure." There were multiple times when her mother made comments about how she did not measure up to her sister, which she recorded as evidence that supports her belief of being a failure. She follows this up with a "BUT" statement (other reasons, other than being a failure that her mother made these comments) that this was only her mother's opinion and that these comments may have been inappropriate and were certainly unhelpful for a parent to express.*

On the right-hand side of the worksheet, instruct group members to write down any evidence that contradicts the core belief. In the next column, after considering all the evidence, they will generate a new, more helpful, less negative, more positive core belief. Return to the example:

> *In the example, the depressed women cites various things that suggest she is, indeed, at least partially successful and certainly not a total failure. After considering the evidence for her core belief with "BUT" statements and after considering the evidence against her core belief, the woman generates a new, more realistic, helpful core belief, "I perform most things I do very well, but, like most people, I do not reach my top goal all of the time." She believes this new belief 95%.*

Instruct group members to rate how much they believe their new beliefs from 0 to 100%. Tell them that just like they should believe in their rational responses, they should also highly believe their new core beliefs. Finally, they will re-rate how much they believe in their original core belief from 0 to 100%. They should see a decrease here from their initial rating. If they don't, they will probably want to add more evidence to review. Go back to the metaphor of chipping away more and more at the iceberg.

Homework (2 min)

✎ Have group members continue with their Weekly Pleasant Activities Plans.

✎ Have group members continue to complete all the columns of the Thought Diary—7 Column form on a daily basis.

✎ Have group members keep looking for themes and patterns in their automatic thoughts to give them more ideas about what their core beliefs are.

✎ Have group members complete the Core Belief Worksheet and be prepared to talk about this process with the group in the next session.

✎ Have group members review Session 10 of the workbook.

✎ Have group members read the overview of Session 11.

Chapter 13 | Session 11: Maintaining Your Gains and Relapse Prevention

(Corresponds to session 11 of the workbook)

Materials Needed

- Personal Goal Planning Sheet
- Nametags
- Flip chart or writing board
- Copy of client workbook

Outline

- Set agenda (2 min)
- Review content of Sessions 9 and 10 (3 min)
- Review homework (40 min)
- Discuss how to maintain gains (10 min)
- Introduce relapse prevention (5 min)
- Give tips for relapse prevention (20 min)
- Discuss setting new personal goals (5 min)
- Assign homework (5 min)

Setting the Agenda (2 min)

Begin the session by setting the agenda and writing it on the flip chart. Refer to the outline at the beginning of this chapter and add any other topics particular to the group.

Review of Sessions 9 and 10 (3 min)

Review the concept of core beliefs. Emphasize the following points:

1. Core beliefs occur at a very deep, higher level of thinking. Core beliefs are different from automatic thoughts (or the words that actually go through our minds) in that they are less conscious.

2. We learn both positive and negative core beliefs based on the experiences we have had in life from childhood to the present. For most of their lives, most people tend to have positive core beliefs. When people become depressed, their negative core beliefs tend to surface.

3. During winter, negative core beliefs are activated among people with SAD. Once negative core beliefs are activated, they influence a person's automatic thoughts, making them more negative.

Homework Review (40 min)

Weekly Pleasant Activities Plan

Ask how group members are doing with planning and carrying out pleasant activities and balancing them with responsibilities. Modify plans as needed. Encourage members to add more activities or increase the amount of time spent on activities.

Thought Diary

Get examples of rational responses from the group and discuss how they impact mood and the degree of belief in the original automatic thought.

Core Belief Worksheet

Elicit examples of what the process of evaluating and changing core beliefs was like. Check that all participants were able to generate "BUT" statements and new, more realistic core beliefs. Discuss any difficulties with the process.

Remind the group that core beliefs are like an iceberg-sized thought. We really believe them to be true, so evaluating and changing them can be difficult and takes time; we have to keep chipping away at the iceberg. Encourage participants to keep working through their core beliefs until, eventually, they get through the process of evaluating and changing all the negative core beliefs they have.

Maintaining Your Gains (10 min)

Tell participants that you hope that they have experienced some improvements in their SAD symptoms and in their quality of life since they started attending this group 5 weeks ago. However, there are still a number of weeks of winter left and it is important for group members to maintain the gains they have made. Use the following dialogue to introduce the concept of maintenance:

> At the beginning of the group, we told you to think of this group as your driving instructor. Just like a driving instructor teaches you the basic skills necessary to be a good driver, this group was meant to teach you some basic skills to cope with winter more effectively. Although it's true that the group is not going to meet anymore after this week, you don't need to stop "driving." You now have the knowledge for how to drive on your own. You are in the driver's seat, so to speak, for coping with your SAD.

Explain to group members that maintaining gains involves asking themselves several questions:

- "What can I do to maintain the gains I've made in this group?"

- "What can I do to make sure I continue to improve even more after the group stops meeting?"

- "Is this as good as it's going to get for me during the winter with my SAD or do I want to try and make it even better?"

- "If I want it to be even better, what can I do to try and make this happen?"

Stress to participants that it is best to think about maintaining gains ahead of time and have a plan in place for how to do it. They might be tempted to just "play it by ear" or "see what happens." However, if these strategies don't work, they may find themselves back in the depths of a SAD episode with no plan for how to get out of it. People who are successful at making a major life change (e.g., quitting smoking or drinking alcohol, or losing weight) tend to have a plan in place for how to maintain their gains. Conclude the discussion with the following dialogue:

> We have asked you to make a major life change in this group—to change your old habits (the ways you used to cope with winter) to more helpful, adaptive ways of coping with winter. If you don't plan ahead, you may fall back into your old habits that contributed to making your SAD worse (e.g., low activity level and negative thinking).

Introduction to Relapse Prevention (5 min)

Use the example of a forest ranger firefighter to introduce the concept of relapse prevention:

> What is a forest ranger firefighter's job? To sit on top of a tower and monitor the forest for signs of a fire. Why do they do that? Chances are good that a forest fire will occur sooner or later (e.g., when the weather is dry, when someone gets careless). The goal of the forest ranger firefighter is then to identify fires quickly, have a plan in place, and put the fire out. This is similar to the position you are in now (or will be in once your SAD improves)—you've got to watch out for future SAD episodes. This is called relapse prevention.

Emphasize the importance of having a relapse prevention plan in place. After all, we cannot prevent winter from happening; winter will recur year after year. A good relapse prevention plan will help participants be ready for winter next time it rolls around so they'll be prepared to cope with it. Inform the group that people who have had repeated SAD episodes in the past are actually at greater risk for SAD episodes, and for depression in general, in the future, which makes relapse prevention especially important.

Have the group recall that in the first week, you told them that cognitive-behavioral therapy (CBT) has been found to be more effective than other types of therapy in preventing relapse.

Reiterate that people who successfully complete CBT are less likely to have future episodes of depression. We expect that this is because people who go through CBT continue to use the skills they learned to cope with stress and changes in mood. Stress that only if they continue to use the skills they have learned in this group can they expect some improvements in how they cope with future fall or winter seasons. If they go back to their old habits and ways of coping, they will likely fall back into the same patterns and experience SAD again.

Tips for Relapse Prevention (20 min)

1. **Be alert to signs and symptoms of SAD.**
   Remind group members that they know what to watch out for—the signs and symptoms of SAD. They should monitor their mood on a regular basis. They can ask themselves, "How have I been feeling over the past week? How have I been handling things lately?" If they notice they are falling back into some of the same old negative patterns (e.g., low energy, sleep problems, negative thinking, do not feel like doing anything, appetite changes), this should alert them.

2. **Take early action.**
   Group members will need to identify any changes in their moods and behaviors, have a plan in place, and take action before they are feeling so badly that they cannot get motivated to do anything about it. Emphasize that they should try to identify early signs of SAD and depression because prevention is easier than treatment for a full-blown SAD episode.

3. **Be aware that major life events can set you up for depression.**
   Mention that people with a history of SAD are also more vulnerable to depression, in general, at any time of the year. Major life events often come before depression so it is important for

group members to be aware of this. Negative life events can occur at any time of the year and often lead to depression. If a major stressful life event were to happen during winter, it could serve as a "double whammy," making SAD worse. Group members should think ahead about ways stressful events may affect them. They will need to monitor their moods more closely when they are under stress and prepare for these events with a plan. Give examples of life events associated with depression:

- *Social separations*: moving away from loved ones or loved ones relocating, divorce or separation or end of a relationship, death of a loved one, etc.
- *Health-related problems*: injury or illness, a new medical problem, etc.
- *New responsibilities and adjustments:* change in career, becoming a caretaker for someone, going back to school, etc.
- *Work-related changes*: promotion, getting laid off, etc.
- *Financial and material changes:* decrease in income, cutting back on spending, etc.

4. **Have a relapse prevention plan in place.**
   Ask group members what strategies would improve their moods if they had a relapse (i.e., if they begin to experience SAD symptoms again next fall or winter). Discuss how they can remind themselves to use what they have learned in this group if they start feeling down again. Elicit other ideas that may help them cope with winter (other than things they have learned in this group).

   Therapist Note
   - *If taking trips South comes up, be sure to discuss the consequences of that: immediate positive consequence (i.e., individuals with SAD typically feel better when they travel South in the winter) versus delayed negative consequence (i.e., upon returning home, a crash is common due to the sudden contrast in climate).* ∎

5. **Remember that your thoughts play a role in relapse and relapse prevention.**
   Group members need to be careful of negative thoughts that can get in the way (e.g., "I must be a failure. I went through this SAD treatment program and I'm depressed in the winter again."). They

should replace these with positive, empowering thoughts (e.g., "I can do something to help myself feel better. I can increase my activity level and work on making my thoughts more positive.").

Setting New Goals (5 min)

Tell the group that we can think of coping more effectively with winter as making a major life change. After all, their old ways of coping with winter were well-formed habits that may have become "comfortable" in some ways. Sometimes making one positive life change can lead to other positive life changes in other areas. Encourage participants to keep the positive momentum going.

Now that they have worked hard to improve their SAD, they may want to generate new goals for themselves. Such goals can include:

- *Individual goals*: educational plans, vocational choices, exercise and physical activity level, economic pursuits, recreational and creative activities

- *Interpersonal goals*: goals related to family, friends, and romantic relationships; joining a group; becoming a leader

Have group members begin to generate short- and long-term goals and record these on the Personal Goal Planning Sheet in the workbook.

Homework (5 min)

✎ Have group members come up with a personal plan for maintaining any gains they have made in this group and for coping with future fall or winter seasons.

✎ Have group members think about any other areas of their lives they would like to change for the better and generate goals.

✎ Instruct group members to use the Personal Goal Planning Sheet to develop their plans and goals and be prepared to share these with the group at the last meeting.

✎ Have group members review Session 11 of the workbook.

✎ Have group members read the overview of Session 12.

Chapter 14 | *Session 12: Review and Farewell*

(Corresponds to session 12 of the workbook)

Materials Needed

- Nametags
- Flip chart or writing board
- Copy of client workbook

Goals

- Set agenda (2 min)
- Review the past 5 weeks (30 min)
- Review homework (35 min)
- Encourage group members to reflect and share comments about the group (20 min)
- Bring the group to a close (3 min)

Setting the Agenda (2 min)

Begin the session by setting the agenda and writing it on the flip chart. Refer to the outline at the beginning of this chapter and add any other topics particular to the group.

As you have given group members a lot of information over the past 5 weeks, it is often helpful to end the group with a summary and review of what has been covered. This can help to refresh participant's memories and see the big picture of what they have learned. Organize the review around important things you hope group members will take with them and remember. You may find the following summaries helpful:

1. SAD and SAD symptoms are a very common experience. SAD is a clinical depression that follows a seasonal pattern of onset (in the fall and winter) and remission (in the spring and summer). SAD prevalence increases with latitude. In general in the United States, the farther away from the equator, the higher the prevalence of SAD and SAD symptoms. SAD symptoms happen on a continuum, where most people experience some changes in mood and behavior during fall and winter. Those with mild-to-moderate SAD symptoms are said to have subsyndromal SAD or S-SAD.

2. SAD symptoms fall into four main categories—physical, emotional, cognitive, and behavioral. (Ask for examples from each category.) These different types of SAD symptoms interact or influence each other in a depressive cycle that could start with any symptom. Each year, SAD episodes actually start with the appearance of one or two symptoms. These one or two symptoms alone may be unpleasant, but manageable. These few early symptoms then lead to the development of more and more symptoms until a person has many symptoms of SAD and feels overwhelmed by them. We call this the vicious SAD cycle, which works to keep SAD symptoms going and gets in the way of feeling better.

3. Our level of pleasant activities relates to how we feel, and doing more can make us feel better. Week 2 focused on skills that could help us feel better on the behavioral level. A high frequency of pleasant activities is associated with satisfaction and happiness. A low frequency of pleasant activities is associated with depressed mood. Activity level and mood act in a negative cycle, where feeling depressed can cause a person to engage in fewer pleasant

activities and becoming less active can cause a person to feel more depressed and so on. The negative mood–activity cycle can start with either depressed mood or a decrease in activity level. To break the negative cycle we must start a positive mood–activity level cycle, where we do a few more pleasant activities and then feel better, which makes us want to do even more activities and so on.

4. What we think about relates to how we feel, and changing unhelpful, negative thoughts into more positive ones can make us feel better. Weeks 3, 4, and 5 focused on skills that could help us feel better on the cognitive level. During Week 3, the A-B-C model showed us how different people can have different reactions to the same situation. We defined thoughts at stage B as automatic thoughts—spontaneous thoughts that just pop into our heads. Automatic thoughts can be positive or negative. Negative automatic thoughts tend to fall into certain categories called cognitive distortions. Cognitive distortions are unhelpful ways of thinking that are common in depression, which tend to make a person feel even worse.

5. In Week 4, we learned how to evaluate our automatic thoughts using the Socratic method. This process involved reviewing the evidence for and against the automatic thought, thinking about the worst/best/most realistic outcome, and problem-solving about the situation that brought on our negative thinking. Then, we added a D to the A-B-C model. D = dispute (change the automatic thought to a rational response). We practiced generating a new, more realistic and helpful thought (a rational response) to replace the original automatic thought. A good rational response is one that we highly believe and that reduces any negative emotions we feel.

6. During Week 5, we began talking about core beliefs. Core beliefs are basic ideas we have about ourselves, other people, and the world in general. Our core beliefs are learned during childhood and are much deeper and less conscious than our automatic thoughts. We worked to identify our core beliefs by looking for patterns or themes in our Thought Diaries. Then, we began to work on evaluating and changing our core beliefs using the Core

Beliefs Worksheet (reviewing the evidence for and against it and coming up with a new, more realistic core belief).

7. Hopefully, even though we did not directly target the emotional and physical symptoms, we experienced some change in those symptoms, too. We should feel less depressed following a pleasant activity, after evaluating negative thoughts, and after thinking rational responses. Activity scheduling should give us a little more energy and focusing on positive rather than negative thoughts should take attention away from any negative physical states (pain, fatigue).

8. In Session 11, we emphasized the importance of having a plan in place for how we will maintain any gains we have made in treatment and prevent relapse. We also broadened our perspective a bit to think about other life areas we may like to improve upon. As with any other lifestyle change (quitting smoking or drinking, losing weight, going through rehab for some health problem, etc.), improving SAD symptoms will take time and effort. We have to keep practicing and building on the skills we have learned to make a difference in our lives.

Homework Review (35 min)

For the last homework assignment, you asked group members to complete the Personal Goal Planning Sheet. Members should have developed their own personalized plans for how to maintain any gains they have made in this group for the rest of this winter, how to cope with future fall–winter seasons to make the seasons even better for them, and how to improve any other areas of their lives. Have group members share some of their goals and plans with each other.

Reflection and Group Sharing (20 min)

Tell participants that sometimes when a therapy group is coming to a close, it is helpful to share any feelings group members have about the group with one another. Give each group member the opportunity to share comments about the group. The following questions can be used to encourage discussion:

- *Out of the skills that you've learned, which have been most helpful to you?*

- *What do you see as the biggest change you've made from this group?*

- *What do you think is left to improve upon?*

- *Who is responsible for any improvements you've made in this group? Is it the group, the group therapists, or you? Or maybe it's that the days are getting longer and warmer?*

People with SAD tend to do the opposite of personalization when it comes to explaining their improvement. For example, a participant might say, "I felt better because the group was helpful or because spring is on its way." Remind participants about their own involvement in their improvement. Use the following dialogue for reinforcement:

Remember, you didn't just sit here passively and listen to the material. You interacted with the group, asked questions, thought about the material between sessions, and did a homework assignment after every session. Even though other factors may be partially related to any improvements you've made, you deserve the majority of the credit. Don't discount your own contribution to your feeling better.

Group Closing (3 min)

At the end of the session, congratulate group members on completing the program. Have them say their good-byes and answer any remaining questions. Emphasize that it is important for them to keep practicing the skills learned in group on their own. Remind them to review their workbooks and seek out additional resources as needed (see suggestions in the workbook).

Fidelity Checklists

Session 1: Introduction to the Group

Fidelity Checklist

Group: _____   Date: _____

Rate your fidelity to each session element on a scale of 1 to 7, with 1 indicating poor fidelity and 7 indicating high fidelity.

Actual Time:

___Set agenda (5 min)   _____

___Introduce group leaders and members (15 min)   _____

___Review the goals of this group (15 min)   _____

___Explain the purpose of this group (5 min)   _____

___Discuss the issue of confidentiality (5 min)   _____

___Introduce cognitive-behavioral therapy (15 min)   _____

___Discuss changes that the group members can expect to make (15 min)   _____

___Present the rationale for homework (10 min)   _____

___Assign homework (5 min)   _____

Notes:

_____

_____

_____

_____

_____

_____

_____

Session 2: Symptoms, Prevalence, and Causes of SAD

Fidelity Checklist

Group: _____   Date: _____

Rate your fidelity to each session element on a scale of 1 to 7, with 1 indicating poor fidelity and 7 indicating high fidelity.

Actual Time:

___Set agenda (2 min)   _____

___Review content of Session 1 (5 min)   _____

___Discuss SAD and its symptoms (40 min)   _____

___Introduce the vicious cycle of SAD symptoms (10 min)   _____

___Explain the prevalence of SAD (5 min)   _____

___Present possible causes of SAD (15 min)   _____

___Discuss the importance of psychological factors in maintaining SAD
(10 min)   _____

___Assign homework (3 min)   _____

Notes:

_____

_____

_____

_____

_____

_____

Session 3: How Activities Relate to Mood and Thoughts

Fidelity Checklist

Group: _____   Date: _____

Rate your fidelity to each session element on a scale of 1 to 7, with 1 indicating poor fidelity and 7 indicating high fidelity.

                                                                    Actual Time:

___Set agenda (2 min)   _____

___Review content of Session 2 (5 min)   _____

___Review Pleasant Activities Rating Scale homework (20 min)   _____

___Discuss pleasant activities and how they relate to mood and thoughts
(25 min)   _____

___Teach the group how to reverse the depressed mood–activity level
cycle (5 min)   _____

___Teach the group how to change thoughts in order to increase activity
level (10 min)   _____

___Help group members choose positive self-statements and plan a
pleasant activity (20 min)   _____

___Assign homework (3 min)   _____

Notes:

_____

_____

_____

_____

_____

_____

Session 4: Doing More to Feel Better

Fidelity Checklist

Group: _____   Date: _____

Rate your fidelity to each session element on a scale of 1 to 7, with 1 indicating poor fidelity and 7 indicating high fidelity.

Actual Time:

___Set agenda (2 min)   _____

___Review content of Session 3 (3 min)   _____

___Review pleasant activities completed for homework (20 min)   _____

___Discuss important mood-related activities (5 min)   _____

___Review possible problems in doing pleasant activities (10 min)   _____

___Discuss how to get started on a balanced activity plan (8 min)   _____

___Review strategies for creating balance (10 min)   _____

___Introduce steps to activity scheduling (10 min)   _____

___Have group members create an activity plan (20 min)   _____

___Assign homework (2 min)   _____

Notes:

_____

_____

_____

_____

_____

_____

_____

_____

Session 5: What You Think Influences How You Feel

Fidelity Checklist

Group: _____   Date: _____

Rate your fidelity to each session element on a scale of 1 to 7, with 1 indicating poor fidelity and 7 indicating high fidelity.

Actual Time:

___Set agenda (2 min)   _____

___Review content of Sessions 3 and 4 (5 min)   _____

___Review homework (20 min)   _____

___Discuss the relationship between thought and mood (10 min)   _____

___Present the A-B-C model (10 min)   _____

___Review events that may cause negative thinking (10 min)   _____

___Introduce the concept of automatic thoughts (10 min)   _____

___Teach group members how to use a thought diary (20 min)   _____

___Assign homework (3 min)   _____

Notes:

_____

_____

_____

_____

_____

_____

_____

Session 6: Cognitive Distortions

Fidelity Checklist

Group: _____   Date: _____

Rate your fidelity to each session element on a scale of 1 to 7, with 1 indicating poor fidelity and 7 indicating high fidelity.

Actual Time:

___Set agenda (2 min)   _____

___Review content of Session 5 (5 min)   _____

___Review homework (40 min)   _____

___Discuss SAD-specific automatic thoughts (10 min)   _____

___Introduce cognitive distortions (15 min)   _____

___Have group members practice identifying cognitive distortions
     (15 min)   _____

___Assign homework (3 min)   _____

Notes:

_____

_____

_____

_____

_____

_____

_____

_____

_____

Session 7: Evaluating Your Automatic Thoughts

Fidelity Checklist

Group: _____   Date: _____

Rate your fidelity to each session element on a scale of 1 to 7, with 1 indicating poor fidelity and 7 indicating high fidelity.

Actual Time:

___Set agenda (2 min)   _____

___Review content of Session 6 (5 min)   _____

___Review homework (30 min)   _____

___Discuss how to evaluate thoughts (2 min)   _____

___Introduce the Automatic Thought Questioning Form (8 min)   _____

___Discuss examples of questioning thoughts (40 min)   _____

___Assign homework (3 min)   _____

Notes:

_____

_____

_____

_____

_____

_____

_____

_____

_____

_____

Session 8: Rational Responses

Fidelity Checklist

Group: _____   Date: _____

Rate your fidelity to each session element on a scale of 1 to 7, with 1 indicating poor fidelity and 7 indicating high fidelity.

Actual Time:

___Set agenda (2 min)   _____

___Review content of Session 7 (5 min)   _____

___Review homework (30 min)   _____

___Teach how to generate rational responses (10 min)   _____

___Discuss the importance of believing in one's rational response (5 min) _____

___Evaluate the impact of rational responses (5 min)   _____

___Discuss examples of rational responses (30 min)   _____

___Assign homework (3 min)   _____

Notes:

_____

_____

_____

_____

_____

_____

_____

_____

Session 9: Core Beliefs

Fidelity Checklist

Group: _____   Date: _____

Rate your fidelity to each session element on a scale of 1 to 7, with 1 indicating poor fidelity and 7 indicating high fidelity

Actual Time:

___Set agenda (2 min)   _____

___Review content of Session 8 (5 min)   _____

___Review homework (50 min)   _____

___Introduce core beliefs (10 min)   _____

___Discuss the difference between core beliefs and automatic thoughts
    (10 min)   _____

___Have group practice identifying core beliefs (10 min)   _____

___Assign homework (3 min)   _____

Notes:

_____

_____

_____

_____

_____

_____

_____

_____

_____

_____

Session 10: Evaluating Your Core Beliefs

Fidelity Checklist

Group: _____   Date: _____

Rate your fidelity to each session element on a scale of 1 to 7, with 1 indicating poor fidelity and 7 indicating high fidelity.

Actual Time:

___Set agenda (2 min)   _____

___Review content of Session 9 (3 min)   _____

___Review homework (40 min)   _____

___Identify core beliefs (30 min)   _____

___Discuss evaluating and changing core beliefs (3 min)   _____

___Introduce the Core Belief Worksheet (10 min)   _____

___Assign homework (2 min)   _____

Notes:

_____

_____

_____

_____

_____

_____

_____

_____

_____

_____

Session 11: Maintaining Your Gains and Relapse Prevention

Fidelity Checklist

Group: _____   Date: _____

Rate your fidelity to each session element on a scale of 1 to 7, with 1 indicating poor fidelity and 7 indicating high fidelity.

Actual Time:

___Set agenda (2 min)   _____

___Review content of Sessions 9 and 10 (3 min)   _____

___Review homework (40 min)   _____

___Discuss how to maintain gains (10 min)   _____

___Introduce relapse prevention (5 min)   _____

___Give tips for relapse prevention (20 min)   _____

___Discuss setting new personal goals (5 min)   _____

___Assign homework (5 min)   _____

Notes:

_____

_____

_____

_____

_____

_____

_____

_____

Session 12: Review and Farewell

Fidelity Checklist

Group: _____

Date: _____

Rate your fidelity to each session element on a scale of 1 to 7, with 1 indicating poor fidelity and 7 indicating high fidelity.

Actual Time:

___Set agenda (2 min) _____

___Review the past 5 weeks (30 min) _____

___Review homework (35 min) _____

___Encourage group members to reflect and share comments about the group (20 min) _____

___Bring the group to a close (3 min) _____

Notes:

_____

_____

_____

_____

_____

_____

_____

_____

_____

_____

_____

_____

References

American Psychiatric Association. (2000). *Diagnostic and statistical manual of mental disorders, fourth edition, text revision* (DSM-IV-TR). Washington, DC: Author.

Beck, A. T. (1967). *Depression: Clinical, experimental, and theoretical aspects.* New York: Hoeber.

Beck, A. T. (1976). *Cognitive therapy and the emotional disorders.* New York: International Universities Press.

Beck, A. T., Rush, J. A., Shaw, B. F., & Emery, G. (1979). *Cognitive therapy of depression.* New York: Guilford Press.

Beck, A. T., Steer, R. A., & Brown, G. K. (1996). *Beck depression inventory—2nd edition manual.* San Antonio, TX: The Psychological Corporation.

Beck, J. S. (1995). *Cognitive-therapy: Basics and beyond.* New York: Guilford Press.

Blackburn, I. M., Eunson, K. M., & Bishop, S. (1986). A two-year naturalistic follow-up of depressed patients treated with cognitive therapy, pharmacotherapy and a combination of both. *Journal of Affective Disorders, 10,* 67–75.

Blazer, D. G., Kessler, R. C., & Schwartz, M. S. (1998). Epidemiology of recurrent major and minor depression with a seasonal pattern: The National Comorbidity Survey. *British Journal of Psychiatry, 172,* 164–167.

Booker, J. M., & Hellekson, C. J. (1992). Prevalence of seasonal affective disorder in Alaska. *American Journal of Psychiatry, 149,* 1176–1182.

Burns, D. D. (1999). *Feeling good: The new mood therapy: The clinically proven drug-free treatment for depression* (Revised and Updated ed.). New York: Avon Books.

Carlsson, A., Svennerholm, L., & Winblad, B. (1980). Seasonal and circadian monoamine variations in human brains examined post mortem. *Acta Psychiatrica Scandinavica, 61* (Suppl. 680), 75–85.

Evans, M. D., Hollon, S. D., DeRubeis, R. J., Piasecki, J. M., Grove, W. M., Garvey, M. J., et al. (1992). Differential relapse following cognitive therapy and pharmacotherapy for depression. *Archives of General Psychiatry, 49* , 802–808.

Gloaguen, V., Cottraux, J., Cucherat, M., & Blackburn, I. M. (1998). A meta-analysis of the effects of cognitive therapy in depressed patients. *Journal of Affective Disorders, 49* , 59–72.

Golden, R. N., Gaynes, B. N., Ekstrom, R. D., Hamer, R. M., Jacobsen, F. M., Suppes, P., et al. (2005). The efficacy of light therapy in the treatment of mood disorders: A meta-analysis of the evidence. *American Journal of Psychiatry, 162,* 656–662.

Hodges, S., & Marks, M. (1998). Cognitive characteristics of seasonal affective disorder: A preliminary investigation. *Journal of Affective Disorders, 50,* 59–64.

Hollon, S. D., DeRubeis, R. J., Shelton, R. C., Amsterdam, J. D., Salomon, R. M., O'Reardon, J. P., et al.(2005). Prevention of relapse following cognitive therapy vs medications in moderate to severe depression. *Archives of General Psychiatry, 62,* 417–422.

Hollon, S. D., Stewart, M. O., & Strunk, D. (2006). Enduring effects for cognitive behavior therapy in the treatment of depression and anxiety. *Annual Review of Psychology, 57,* 285–315.

Kasper, S., Wehr, T. A., Bartko, J. J., Gaist, P. A., & Rosenthal, N. E. (1989). Epidemiological findings of seasonal changes in mood and behavior: A telephone survey of Montgomery County, Maryland. *Archives of General Psychiatry, 46,* 823–833.

Lam, R. W., & Levitt, A. J. (1999). *Clinical guidelines for the treatment of seasonal affective disorder.* Vancouver, BC: Clinical & Academic Publishing.

Lam, R. W., Tam, E. M., Yatham, L. N., Shiah, I. -S., & Zis, A. P. (2001). Seasonal depression: The dual vulnerability hypothesis revisited. *Journal of Affective Disorders, 63,* 123–132.

Lambert, G. W., Reid, C., Kaye, D. M., Jennings, G. L., & Esler, M. D. (2002). Effect of sunlight and season on serotonin turnover in the brain. *Lancet, 360,* 1840–1842.

Levitan, R. D., Rector, N. A., & Bagby, M. (1998). Negative attributional style in seasonal affective disorder. *American Journal of Psychiatry, 155,* 428–430.

Lewinsohn, P. M. (1974). A behavioral approach to depression. In R. J. Friedman & M. M. Katz (Eds.), *The psychology of depression:*

Contemporary theory and research (pp. 157–178). Washington, DC: John Wiley & Sons.

MacPhillamy, D. J., & Lewinsohn, P. M. (1982). The pleasant events schedule: Studies on reliability, validity, and scale intercorrelation. *Journal of Consulting and Clinical Psychology, 50*, 363–380.

Magnusson, A. (2000). An overview of epidemiological studies on seasonal affective disorder. *Acta Psychiatrica Scandinavica, 101*, 176–184.

Magnusson, A., & Partonen, T. (2005). The diagnosis, symptomatology, and epidemiology of seasonal affective disorder. *CNS Spectrums, 10*, 625–634.

Nolen-Hoeksema, S. (1987). Sex differences in unipolar depression: Evidence and theory. *Psychological Bulletin, 101*, 259–282.

Pate, R. R., Pratt, M., Blair, S. N., Haskell, W. L., Macera, C. A., Bouchard, C., et al. (1995). Physical activity and public health: A recommendation from the Centers for Disease Control and Prevention and the American College of Sports Medicine. *Journal of the American Medical Association, 273*, 402–407.

Pinchasov, B. B., Shurgaja, A. M., Grischin, O. V., & Putilov, A. A. (2000). Mood and energy regulation in seasonal and non-seasonal depression before and after midday treatment with physical exercise or bright light. *Psychiatry Research, 94*(1), 29–42.

Rohan, K. J., Roecklein, K. A., Lacy, T. M., & Vacek, P. M. (submitted). Winter depression recurrence one year after cognitive-behavioral therapy, light therapy, or combination treatment.

Rohan, K. J., Roecklein, K. A., Tierney Lindsey, K., Johnson, L. G., Lippy, R. D., Lacy, T. M., et al. (2007). A randomized controlled trial of cognitive-behavioral therapy, light therapy, and their combination for seasonal affective disorder. *Journal of Consulting and Clinical Psychology, 75*, 489–500.

Rohan, K. J., Sigmon, S. T., & Dorhofer, D. M. (2003). Cognitive-behavioral factors in seasonal affective disorder. *Journal of Consulting and Clinical Psychology, 71*, 22–30.

Rohan, K. J., Tierney Lindsey, K., Roecklein, K. A., & Lacy, T. J. (2004). Cognitive-behavioral therapy, light therapy, and their combination in treating seasonal affective disorder. *Journal of Affective Disorders, 80*, 273–283.

Rosen, L. N., Targum, S. D., Terman, M., Bryant, M. J., Hoffman, H., Kasper, S. F., et al. (1990). Prevalence of seasonal affective disorder at four latitudes. *Psychiatry Research, 31*, 131–144.

Rosenthal, N. E., Sack, D. A., Gillin, C., Lewy, A. J., Goodwin, F. K., Davenport, Y., et al. (1984). Seasonal affective disorder: A description of the syndrome and preliminary findings with light therapy. *Archives of General Psychiatry, 41*, 72–80.

Schwartz, P. J., Brown, C., Wehr, T. A., & Rosenthal, N. E. (1996). Winter seasonal affective disorder: A follow-up study of the first 59 patients of the National Institute of Mental Health Seasonal Studies Program. *American Journal of Psychiatry, 153*, 1028–1036.

Simons, A. D., Murphy, G. E., Levine, J. L., & Wetzel, R. D. (1986). Cognitive therapy and pharmacotherapy for depression: Sustained improvement over one year. *Archives of General Psychiatry, 43*, 43–38.

Terman, M., Terman, J. S., Quitkin, F., McGrath, P., Stewart, J., & Rafferty, B. (1989). Light therapy for seasonal affective disorder: A review of efficacy. *Neuropsychopharmacology, 2*, 1–22.

Terman, M., Terman, J. S., & Rafferty, B. (1990). Experimental design and measures of success in the treatment of winter depression by bright light. *Psychopharmacology Bulletin, 26*, 505–510.

Wehr, T. A., Duncan, W. C., Jr., Sher, L., Aeschbach, D., Schwartz, P. J., Turner, E. H., et al. (2001). A circadian signal of change of season in patients with seasonal affective disorder. *Archives of General Psychiatry, 58*, 1108–1114.

Weissman, A. N., & Beck, A. T. (1978, November). *Development and validation of the Dysfunctional Attitude Scale.* Paper presented at the meeting of the Association for the Advancement of Behavior Therapy, Chicago, IL.

Westrin, A., & Lam, R. W. (2007). Seasonal affective disorder: A clinical update. *Annals of Clinical Psychiatry, 19*(4), 239–246.

Williams, J. B., Link, M. J., Rosenthal, N. E., Amira, L., & Terman, M. (1992). *Structured interview guide for the hamilton depression rating scale—seasonal affective disorder version (SIGH-SAD).* New York: New York State Psychiatric Institute.

Young, J., & Brown, G. (2003). *Young schema questionnaire (YSQ).* New York: Cognitive Therapy Center of New York. http://www.schematherapy.com/id53.htm

Young, M. A. (1999). Integrating psychological and physiological mechanisms of SAD: The dual-vulnerability model. *Biological Rhythms Bulletin, 1*, 4–6.

Young, M. A., & Azam, O. (2003). Ruminative response style and the severity of seasonal affective disorder. *Cognitive Therapy and Research, 27*, 223–233.

About the Author

Kelly J. Rohan, PhD is Associate Professor of Psychology at the University of Vermont, where she also directs the Mood Disorders Laboratory and Seasonality Treatment Program. She has also been on the faculty of the Uniformed Services University of the Health Sciences in the Department of Medical and Clinical Psychology. Dr. Rohan received her BA from Saint Bonaventure University and her PhD in clinical psychology from the University of Maine. She completed her residency and a 2-year postdoctoral fellowship at the University of Mississippi Medical School/Jackson Veterans Affairs Medical Center Consortium. Dr. Rohan's area of interest is mood disorders, with specialization in seasonal affective disorder (SAD) and cognitive-behavioral treatments. Dr. Rohan has received research funding from the National Institute of Mental Health and was awarded the Young Investigator Research Award from the Society for Light Treatment and Biological Rhythms for her work on cognitive-behavioral therapy for SAD.